HILL 112

By the same author:

Normandy : The British Breakout

HILL 112

Cornerstone of the Normandy Campaign

Major J. J. How, MC

WILLIAM KIMBER · LONDON

First published in 1984 by
WILLIAM KIMBER & CO. LIMITED
100 Jermyn Street, London, SW1Y 6EE

ISBN 0-7183-0540-X

Typeset by Grove Graphics, Tring
and printed in Great Britain by
Redwood Burn Limited, Trowbridge

Contents

List of Maps

List of Illustrations

Acknowledgements

I am grateful to the many who have assisted me in the production of this book. Acknowledgement is made to those who originated eye-witness accounts by naming them either in the text or in a footnote to which attention is drawn by an asterisk. Rank, where given, is that at the time of the battle. To those who have discussed these battles with me personally or in correspondence and who may recognise in the text information to which they have contributed I am also grateful. My particular thanks go to Ernst Streng, Lieutenant-Colonel Steel Brownlie, Heinz Damaske (Frundsberg Suchdienst) and John Thorpe who have allowed me to quote from diaries and unpublished accounts of battles. I am grateful to Paul Hocking for his help with formation signs and other graphical work.

I am indebted to Dr Jean-Pierre Benamou of the Musée Memorial, Bayeux, to Editions Heimdal, Bayeux, to the Munin Verlag, Osnabrueck, to the Imperial War Museum, London, to the Bundesarchiv, Koblenz, to Herbert Fuerbringer, Hans Höller, Georges Bernage and Mrs Schroif for permission to reproduce photographs.

I acknowledge with thanks permission to quote from the following published works:

Mr Robert Woollcombe, author of *Lion Rampant*; Major Noel Bell, author of *From the Beaches to the Baltic*; Hauptmann Will Fey, a.D., author of *Panzer im Brennpunkt der Fronten*; the Munin Verlag, Osnabrueck, *Kriegsgeschichte der 12. SS-Panzerdivision 'Hitlerjugend'* by Hubert Meyer; Presses de la Cité, Paris, *La Bataille du Calvados* by Albert Grandais; General Sir Cecil Blacker, *The Story of the 23rd Hussars*; Cassell Ltd, *Closing the Ring* by Winston Churchill; Souvenir Press Ltd, London, *Caen: Anvil of Victory* by Alexander McKee; the Regimental Association of the Royal Regiment of Wales, *History of the South Wales Borderers & The Monmouthshire Regiment Vol III*

1933–1945 by G. A. Brett and *The History of the Welch Regiment 1919–1951* by Lomax and de Courcy; the Light Infantry (Cornwall) Regimental Association, *The Duke of Cornwall's Light Infantry 1939–1945*; the Light Infantry (Somerset) Regimental Association, *History of the 4th Bn The Somerset Light Infantry (Prince Albert's) in the Campaign in North-West Europe June 1944–1945*; Wilding & Son (Redverse Ltd), Shrewsbury, *History of the 4th Battalion King's Shropshire Light Infantry (TA) (1745–1945)*; the Regimental Association of the King's Own Scottish Borderers, *The 6th (Border) Battalion The King's Own Scottish Borderers 1939–1945*; the 2nd Northamptonshire Yeomanry Association, *The History of the Northamptonshire Yeomanry* by Bevan; Oxford University Press, *War Report* ed. Cumberlege; and to published and unpublished works not shown above but which are listed in the *Source References* at the end of the book.

CHAPTER ONE

Call to Combat at Caen

'Fighting in the Caen streets!' The newspaper headlines screamed out at the reader. It was 7th June 1944. British and American troops had gained a foothold on the beaches of Normandy. But 'Fighting in the Caen streets'? Truth, alas had been swept aside. Relief and euphoria had swamped the country. Four long years of waiting had created its own optimism. And the sea had not run with blood, as Churchill in his worst moments had feared, the paratroopers had not been annihilated as the Allied Air Commander had foretold. That Caen had not been taken on the first day as planned seemed of minor importance. But General Bernard Montgomery wanted Caen.

Caen was the key road and rail centre in Normandy. It also happened to be the boundary between the two German armies defending northern France; its fall would threaten to drive a wedge between them. It would be pointing a finger at Paris. That is why Montgomery was so determined to take it: that is why his old opponent in the desert, Field-Marshal Rommel, was determined he shouldn't get it. Rommel had read the intention even before the invasion took place. That is why he had placed the 21st Panzer Division to bar the way. And when a second panzer division arrived, the 12th SS Hitler Youth, he had placed that there, too. The pattern for the battle for Normandy had been set. Caen was the challenge to combat. Caen was the magnet that would attract the powerful German armour and hold it away from the Americans while they captured Cherbourg, the essential port, and prepared to break out in the west.

Montgomery had tried to take Caen with his 3rd Division on the first day of the invasion. These were the regulars he commanded with such skill four years earlier at Dunkirk. He next sent in the Canadians, a fighting élite, all volunteers. They fought themselves to a standstill in the face of men as brave as themselves, as aggressive and determined, the Hitler Youth Division. Montgomery then fell back on his veterans of the desert, the men with sand in their shoes, the battle-hardened soldiers he had insisted should be amongst the first to land in Normandy. His plan was to encircle Caen with a pincer movement that was to be locked shut with an airborne drop from England. Disaster! The 51st Highland Division failed to make any appreciable progress in the east, the famous Desert Rats were thrown back after a brief 'swan' in the west, and the airborne division never left England. Left behind to rust on the road out of Villers Bocage was the British armoured spearhead. Fifty-three fighting vehicles shot into scrap in a sudden encounter with four German Tiger tanks. Amongst the tangled mass of metal left behind in enemy territory were twenty-five Cromwell tanks.

It signified something more than the failure of Monty's new attempt to take Caen. The Cromwell tank was in battle for the first time. Demolished were the hopes that the British might at last have produced a tank that could stand up to those panzers. A few weeks later the Cromwell was replaced; for the rest of the war the British had to rely on the American Sherman as their main cruiser tank. The top Allied generals were reporting that the Tiger could out-gun any Allied tank in the field and that the Panthers were more than a match for the Shermans. Even before the invasion the British top brass were well aware of the disadvantage their tank crews would be fighting under. They hurried with the conversion of a number of Shermans to take the British seventeen pounder anti-tank gun.* Tank battalions equipped with Shermans received them just in time for the invasion on a scale of one to each troop of four tanks. In Normandy tank crews soon found out for themselves what they were up against. The 23rd Hussars carried out some trials on a knocked-out Panther.

> It was found that a 75-millimetre gun [standard in the Sherman] made no impression on the front at all, unless it was lucky enough to hit the turret ring, a very small target indeed. The 17-pounder was more encouraging . . . for it penetrated the front of the Panther's turret at three hundred yards, though it did not always go through the sloped front plate of the hull . . . we decided that head-on Panthers should be treated with circumspection.[1]

As for Tigers, they resulted in a phobia that produced shouts of 'Tiger!' at the mere glimpse of a German armoured vehicle.

Ten days had passed. The British and Canadians were still held up

* This converted Sherman was called a Firefly.

'The Desert Rats were thrown back . . .' A German artist's impression published in the propaganda magazine *Signal*.

'Fifty-three fighting vehicles shot into scrap.' Some of the destroyed British vehicles on the side of the road leading out of Villers-Bocage.

short of Caen, more or less where they had been since the first day of the invasion. The early optimism was going. The reality of a hard battle in Normandy was sinking in. The Prime Minister felt it necessary to write to the Minister of Information complaining about the use of words like 'brutish' and 'extraordinary stupidity' as descriptive of the German soldier: it '. . . certainly does not extend to their use of their arms or to their seizing of tactical opportunities'.[2]

The grass was no greener on the other side of the hill. Hitler was furious that the Allies had not been thrown straight back into the sea as he had ordered. Rommel's first attempt, with three panzer divisions under Panzer Group West, was literally blown to pieces. The headquarters was attacked from the air wounding the general in command, killing twelve of his staff officers, wounding others and destroying his communications centre. Thereafter, Montgomery's continued pressure pulled in the panzer divisions as they arrived. At the end of the first week there were four of them at the Caen end of the front, and two more on the way. There was not one on the American front further east.

Hitler realised, however, that although sixty German divisions were spread out along the coasts of Holland, Belgium and France, they lacked both the mobility and the armour to deal with the British and Americans concentrated as they were on the Normandy front. He had already decided to get his armoured punch from Russia.

> On 12.6.44 the II SS Panzer Corps with the 9th SS Panzer Division 'Hohenstaufen' and the 10th SS Panzer Division 'Frundsberg' leaves the Army Group of the North Ukraine . . .[3]

Hitler was relying on these men to break the impasse in Normandy. For over a year the forty thousand men of the II SS Panzer Corps had trained in France to throw out the Allied invaders when they came. 'Had they been there the invasion would not have succeeded,' said Hitler later. Alas, the spring daffodils in Normandy had brought crisis in Russia. The II SS Panzer Corps had been rushed east. Now, with the first poppies showing red in the cornfields, they were on their way back. A different set of alarm bells was ringing. But Russia was far away. It would take time – and two hundred locomotives with appropriate rolling stock.

*

'My broad impression is that the enemy is going to make an invasion elsewhere.'

This message, sent by Rommel to Supreme Headquarters in Germany on the second day of the invasion, was in Montgomery's hands soon after. Never before has a general been so privileged to listen in to the thoughts and commands of his opponents. Ultra, the British code breakers, supplied Montgomery and the army commanders subordinate to him with intercepts of all the important top secret radio messages and commands – but not those sent by telephone. Montgomery knew that although sixteen divisions of the German Fifteenth Army were close at hand in the Pas de Calais, they would not be moved against him as long as British intelligence and a battalion of American signallers could continue to persuade the German High Command that an American army – which did not exist – was standing by at Dover and Folkestone, about to cross and land on the beaches in the Calais area. Montgomery received regular information on the dispositions of the German troops, and he knew that the 1st SS Panzer Division was moving from Belgium towards Normandy and that the 2nd SS Panzer Division driving north from the south of France had been held up in Limoges by French partisan activity. He was, as yet, unaware that the II SS Panzer Corps had been ordered back from Russia and was

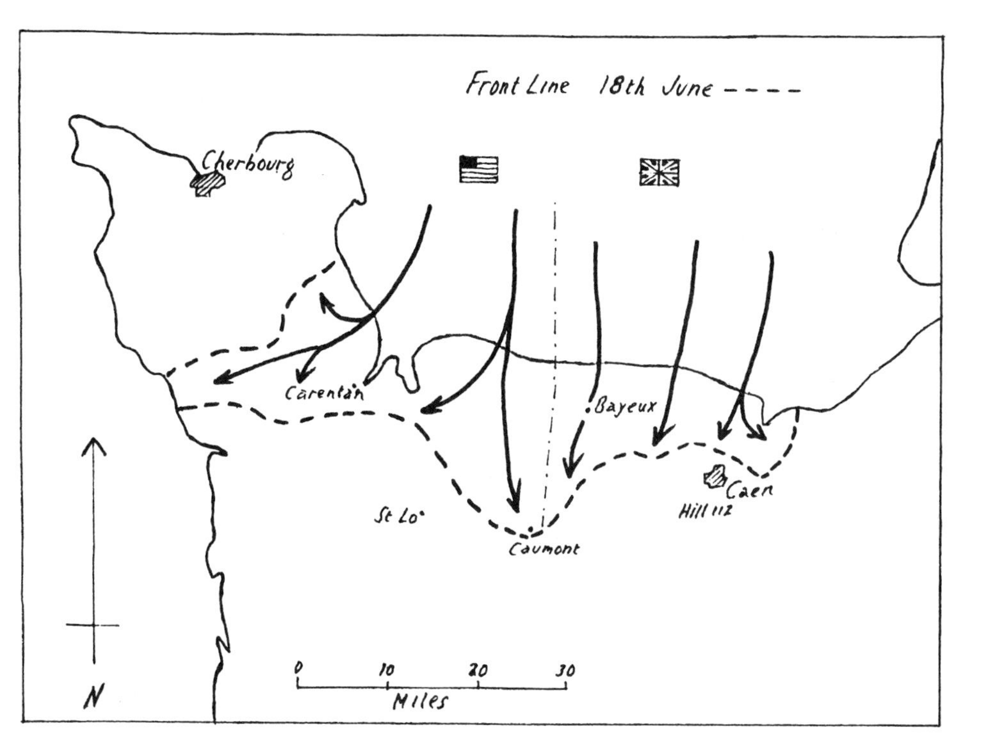

beginning to arrive in France – that involved communications outside the range of Ultra interception.

*

'You must keep the enemy off balance' was one of Montgomery's favourite sayings. He had done just that. And to keep the initiative he would now have to launch some new offensive. On the 18th he issued a new directive to his British and American Army commanders:

> It is clear that we must now capture Caen and Cherbourg. I hope to see both captured by the 24th.

The Americans were already moving on Cherbourg. The British had been trying for twelve days to take Caen. But new divisions were landing. This time he would try with them. But they were not yet complete. The offensive would have to start on the 22nd. On the 19th a storm arose. For three days it grew, it blew and it blustered. Landing craft were thrown upon to the beaches, others sank whilst trying to ride it out at sea. Quays were smashed. Everywhere lay the debris of the storm. Montgomery looked again at directive for the British attack: he crossed out 22nd and pencilled in its place 26th.

VIII CORPS

CHAPTER TWO

Wot! No sand in their shoes!

'We have many troops as yet untried in battle,' said Montgomery in his pre-invasion pep talk to the officers of the British Second Army. 'It is vital to see that they have a good show in their first battle!' These were the British divisions now landing in Normandy. It was the turn of the untried formations to throw themselves into the battle for Caen.

They were the 15th Scottish Division, the 11th Armoured Division, the 43rd Wessex Division and two independent tank brigades, the 4th and 31st. They formed the British VIII Corps under Major-General Richard O'Connor.

'O'Connor is the only general who makes me nervous.' These words, attributed to Rommel, true or not, are a measure of O'Connor's fine reputation. In Britain's darkest hour of defeat he had pulled off an audacious victory in the north African desert. With 31,000 Australian, New Zealand, Indian and United Kingdom troops he had shattered an Italian army of a quarter of a million men, taking 130,000 prisoners and capturing hundreds of guns and tanks. When, later, he was taken prisoner by a German motorised patrol, Churchill is said to have offered any six of the Italian generals to get him back. Apocryphal? Certainly, and like the comment attributed to Rommel, a measure of the man. Alas, the years as a prisoner were years during which O'Connor was passed over. He had, however, escaped – at the second attempt – in time to command the VIII Corps in Normandy.

The divisions of O'Connor's 'White Knight' Corps were made up predominantly of the peace-time week-end soldiers, the territorials. Four years of war had brought changes: older men had been posted, conscripts had taken their place; new commanding officers, regulars, had arrived; but the ethos of these units had remained. They were still closely knit local groups: men of Scotland in regiments like the Ayrshire Yeomanry, Cameronians and Glasgow Highlanders; men from the Welsh border counties of Shropshire, Herefordshire and Monmouthshire; men of Wessex in the Hampshires, Wiltshires, Somerset Light Infantry and other famous west country regiments; there were Cockneys with the Rifle Brigade and men of the Midlands in the Northamptonshire Yeomanry. The years of training had turned them into professionals: at heart they had remained civilians.

They had lived through the long years of a nation at bay. They had sat around the wireless sets in crowded NAAFI canteens to learn of disasters: Norway, Dunkirk, Greece, Hong Kong, Singapore. Each new defeat had brought tougher assault courses, tougher battle schools, and more bloodthirsty exhortations: 'One more in the guts for Singapore!' They had surged forward behind the barrages of live ammunition to shouts of: 'The closer you get the safer you are!' They had learned the new catechism: 'Why won't those Jerry bastards fire back?' – 'Because they've all got their bloody heads down!' They had lived in camps where marching was out and running was in – from six o'clock in the morning until six o'clock in the evening. They had sweated their way through the weekly ten miles in two hours in battle order with weapons and ammunition – and no officers excused. These men had fought the battles of the big exercises: Bumper (1941) and Tiger (1942), the sodden downpours of Blackcock (1943) and the biting blasts of Eagle (1944), February on the bald Yorkshire moors, fighting yet one more battle for the Octon crossroads:

'Well, man, it can't be worse than that – I mean the real thing boyo!'

'No! – No! – But the bullets will be real, see!'

They had made their way back to camp, filthy, exhausted and hungry, the lucky ones in the back of a three-tonner, and voices had poured forth in song: 'She'll be wearing khaki issue . . . ', 'If I were the marrying kind . . . ', and at the sight of a pretty girl a quick change to: 'Why was she born so beautiful . . . ' and then back to that man who could do such wonderful things 'with a dexterous twist of his sinuous wrist.'

One enemy at least – Dr Goebbels, the Minister for Propaganda in Hitler's Germany – was beaten at his own game when one day Monty himself turned up to talk to them in that curiously high-pitched beaky voice, in those sharp, clipped sentences:

'. . . wanted to come . . . have a look at one another . . . job to do . . . RAF now knocking Hun for six . . . then we go over . . . Simple – quite simple! . . . Confidence – that's what's wanted . . . Confidence in our-

Panzer grenadiers of the 12th SS Hitler Youth Panzer Division.

selves . . . Then hand in hand to the final victory . . . easy . . . quite easy . . . not difficult at all.'

And with three loud cheers the Monty travelling show had left, Rolls Royce in the lead, king-size Union Jack fluttering from the bonnet, and the Lord, Almighty in Battle, hovering just above. Who were these men now landing in Normandy? What were their feelings on the eve of Montgomery's new offensive to take Caen? One was Lieutenant Robert Woollcombe of the 7th King's Own Scottish Borderers (15th Scottish Division):

> Esprit de corps at the highest pitch. The troops in amazing spirits. For here was the Second Front. We were upon the rostrum of the world. At last, after months and years of waiting whilst others went out, we too were out, to take part of deeds . . . These were wonderful moments.[4]

Commanding a troop of Sherman tanks with the Fife and Forfar Yeomanry was Lieutenant Steel Brownlie (11th Armoured Division):

> Confidence could be detected everywhere, from the CO right down to the hull gunner. We left Aldershot at some unearthly hour on a dull dank morning, with no farewell but that of our fellows, who in their hearts wanted more than anything else to be with us – the regimental reserve, who were to follow us in a few days and fill the gaps that would no doubt have appeared in our ranks by that time.

Then there was the platoon commander with the 3rd Monmouths (11th Armoured Division) who persuaded the medical officer in charge of the convalescent home to declare him fit so that he could get back to his battalion before the balloon went up:

> I rejoined the battalion at Aldershot, and a few days later we were on our way. On the boat going over Jack France told us that he was going to keep a Mills grenade in each pouch pocket: 'One is for Jerry, and the other is for me if I'm in a tight corner. No bloody German is going to take me prisoner!' He was the only officer in the battalion with previous battle experience. He had come up from the ranks, a regular, and had fought with Montgomery's Division on the retreat to Dunkirk.*

* Major Jack France was killed in action six weeks later.

Operation Epsom was the name Monty gave to the new offensive to take Caen. He was making certain this time, with a total build-up of sixty thousand troops and seven hundred guns. The plan was to pierce a short two-mile stretch of the German front and drive a deep salient into the rear of the city. Threatened with encirclement the enemy would be forced to withdraw.

Only the 15th Scottish and supporting tanks were to be involved in the initial assault, and the front was so restricted that units would be committed progressively as ground was gained. Once the Scotsmen had pierced the crust of the defence, the tanks of 11th Armoured Division were to drive through the corridor, seize two bridges over the Odon, and advance to the high ground (Hill 112) beyond; this was to be repeated, with the salient being driven across the second river, the Orne, and on to the high ground in the rear of Caen. The task of the 43rd Wessex Division was to follow up and take over, holding the ground won and widening the salient.

The enemy holding the front was 12th SS Hitler Youth Panzer Division. On their right was the 21st Panzer Division and on their left was the Panzer Lehr Division. These divisions had been Rommel's counter-attack force. Montgomery had seized the initiative with his

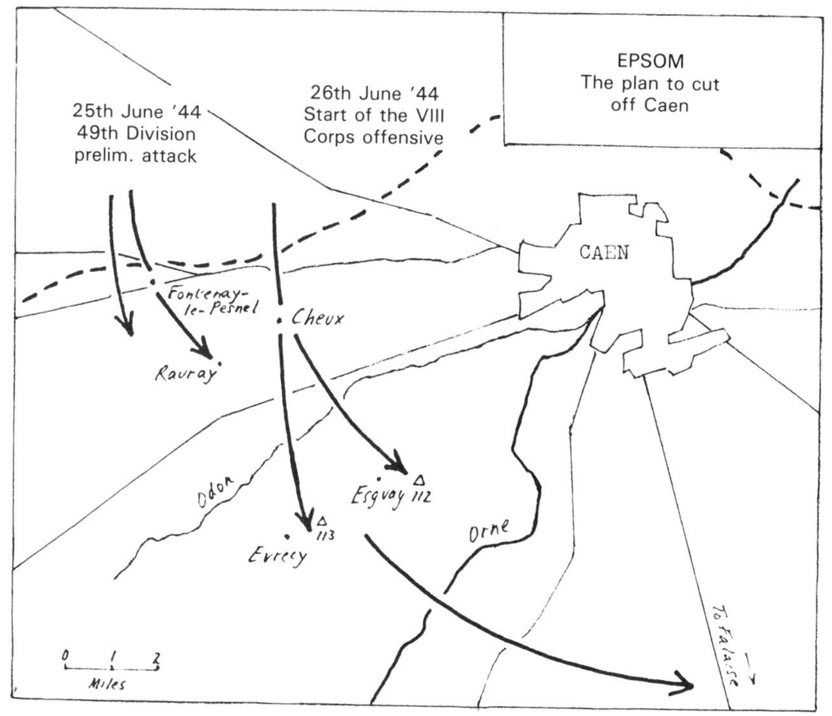

successive attacks. Instead of counter-attacking the panzer divisions had been pulled into the defence and held there.

For eighteen days of stalemate the 3rd Canadian Division had battled fiercely on the front north-west of Caen with the Hitler Youth Division. The Canadians had fought with the bitter memory of the Canadian dead of Dieppe in their souls: the Hitler Youth were steadfast in their faith in Fuehrer and Fatherland. It was not long before the soldiers of both sides were firm in the belief that their opponents were shooting prisoners. Both sides produced evidence and reported it to higher authority. This was a rough and tough battle.

The 12th SS (HY) Panzer Division was formed in 1943 from youths of seventeen and eighteen recruited through the Hitler Youth movement. During training in Belgium and France it became apparent that some had 'volunteered' under pressure. They were allowed to leave and join Wehrmacht formations. There can be no doubt, however, that the majority were full of the reckless audacity and enthusiasm of youth and were eager to see action. Officers and senior NCOs were older men who had proved themselves in battle. Rigid discipline was rejected for a looser relationship relying on youthful ardour, commitment and respect for leaders with experience. The drill ground played no part; the time was given to weapon and field training, with particular emphasis on camouflage, and on defensive and offensive tactics, particularly infiltration. These teenage soldiers were given extra rations to counter the effects of earlier, war-time shortages; those under eighteen were given a sweet ration in lieu of cigarettes. They had gone into battle convinced that their cause was just and that the outcome would be decisive for their country.

A panzer division is essentially an offensive formation. Even with two Grenadier regiments, six battalions of infantry, 12th SS had too few men to hold the twelve-mile front it had been given. The Engineer Battalion had been brought in to hold a sector. Infantry casualties were to cause the Germans to use increasingly their engineers in this role during the Normandy campaign: it was one they were well trained to carry out and which they fully accepted.

It was on a two-mile stretch of that twelve-mile front that the Scottish assault, backed by almost seven hundred guns, was to fall. And bang in the centre of that line of advancing Scotsmen would be the positions of the Hitler Youth Engineer Battalion.

CHAPTER THREE

Prelude to Epsom

25th June 1944

The slip of paper handed to General Montgomery by his Ultra liaison officer on the morning of 24th June must have spoiled even that supremely confident commander's favourite breakfast of 'bubble and squeak'. The British secret service had been eavesdropping again. The II SS Panzer Corps with two powerful panzer divisions, 9th SS and 10th SS, had just arrived on his doorstep from Russia. Seventy-eight trains carrying 9th SS and sixty-two with 10th SS had detrained in Rommel's command area. Some elements were a mere sixty miles from the Normandy battlefield. These were not the only German reinforcements. The 2nd SS Panzer Division, ten days earlier reported held up by the French underground at Limoges, had now arrived and was assembling at Caumont. The 1st SS Panzer Division and a Luftwaffe infantry division, en route from Belgium, were close at hand.

So far Montgomery had succeeded in holding the German armour as it arrived on the Caen front. But soon there would be four more divisions. How was he to hold them? Only by ensuring that VIII Corps was launched into the Epsom offensive without delay. Success there might attract and bind down these new divisions. Montgomery sat down and wrote a telegram to General Eisenhower, the Supreme Commander of the Allied Forces.

> If we can pull the enemy onto [British] Second Army it will make it easier for [American] First Army when it attacks southward.
>
> Once it starts I will continue battling on eastern flank until one of us cracks and it will not be us . . .

On the eve of this battle there came from the Minister of War in the UK an enquiry about depressing reports concerning the inferiority of

(l to r) Lieutenant-General Richard O'Connor, commander of VIII Corps, Lieutenant-General Miles C. Dempsey, commander of the British Second Army, and General Bernard Montgomery, commander of the Allied armies fighting in Normandy.

Field-Marshal Rommel, commander of German Army Group 'B', with officers of the 21st Panzer Division.

British equipment in battle, particularly the failure of the new British tank, the Cromwell. The touch of irritation in Montgomery's reply is understandable:

> We cannot have anything of that sort at this time . . . tomorrow we leap on the enemy. Anything that undermines confidence and morale must be stamped on ruthlessly.

There was, however, also good news. Montgomery had received a copy of this frantic exhortation sent by Hitler to his commander in Cherbourg: '. . . defend to the last pillbox . . . Leave the enemy not a harbour but a field of devastation.' Cherbourg was about to fall to the Americans. The Allies would soon have a major port in their hands.

*

While Montgomery was preparing the major offensive that was to take Caen, Hitler had given the go-ahead for the massed panzer blow that was to throw the Allies out of Normandy. This time there was to be no mistake. It had taken twelve days for the forty thousand men of the II SS Panzer Corps, 9th SS Hohenstaufen and 10th SS Frundsberg, to make the journey from the Russian front. Allied air attack and sabotage by the French underground had forced units to detrain on the French/German border. Some had still to complete the journey by road. Also on the way to Normandy were the 1st SS Adolf Hitler, and the 2nd SS Das Reich Panzer Division.

On 20th June Hitler issued an order giving his generals notice of his intention: '. . . the 1st, 2nd, 9th, 10th SS and the 2nd Panzer and the Panzer Lehr Division are to make a massed counter-attack to destroy, first, the American forces . . .'[5]

Rommel's objection that it would be two weeks before the counter-attack could be mounted, left a Fuehrer angry and fuming about generals who were not prepared to take the necessary risk.

In the days that followed the plans began to take shape:

June 23rd: General of the Waffen SS Paul Hausser announces that his II SS Panzer Corps witth the 9th SS Hohenstaufen and 10th SS Frundsberg panzer divisions will have arrived complete from Russia by the 25th.

June 24th: Panzer General Geyr von Schweppenburg, commander of Panzer Group West, meets with the generals who will be taking part.

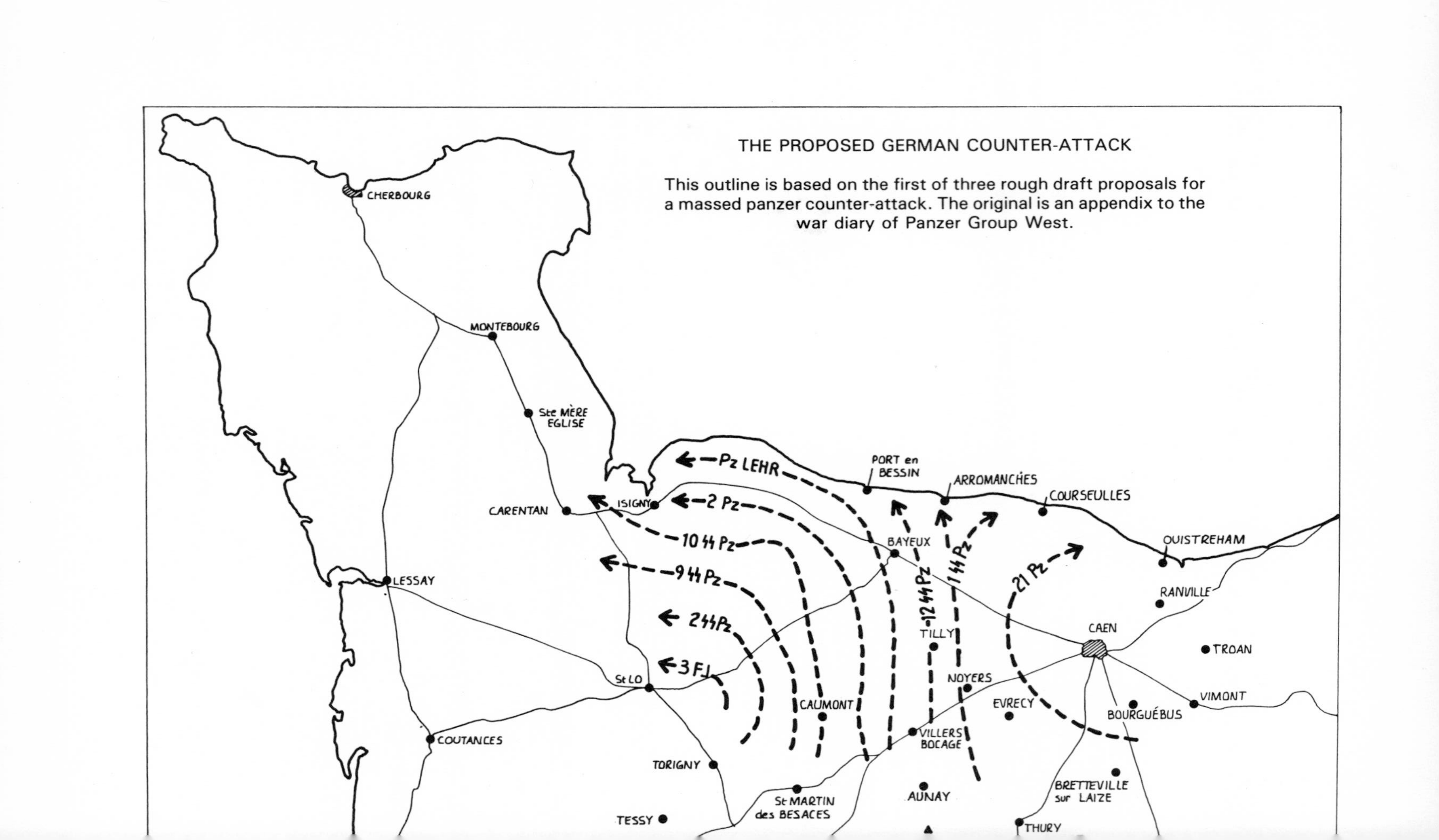
THE PROPOSED GERMAN COUNTER-ATTACK
This outline is based on the first of three rough draft proposals for a massed panzer counter-attack. The original is an appendix to the war diary of Panzer Group West.
CHERBOURG
MONTEBOURG
Ste MÈRE EGLISE
CARENTAN
ISIGNY
LESSAY
COUTANCES
St LO
TORIGNY
TESSY
St MARTIN des BESACES
CAUMONT
VILLERS BOCAGE
AUNAY
TILLY
NOYERS
EVRECY
BAYEUX
PORT en BESSIN
ARROMANCHES
COURSEULLES
OUISTREHAM
RANVILLE
CAEN
TROAN
VIMONT
BOURGUÉBUS
BRETTEVILLE sur LAIZE
THURY
Pz LEHR
2 Pz
10 SS Pz
9 SS Pz
2 SS Pz
3 FJ
12 SS Pz
1 SS Pz
21 Pz

> The counter-attack will be under command of Panzer Group West. It will drive a wedge between the Allied armies. It will then destroy the western wing under the Americans before turning against the British and defeating them also. You are to make the necessary reconnaissance for an attack to go in between Villers Bocage and Caumont.[6]

June 25th: Rommel orders all available transport to speed up the journey of the 276 and 277 Infantry Divisions and the 16th Luftwaffe Field Division. They are still about a hundred and fifty miles away and are urgently required to relieve those panzer divisions at present holding the front.

June 26th: Panzer General Geyr von Schweppenburg issues a secret instruction: the initial attack must be planned to start one hour before nightfall and to continue throughout the hours of darkness.

It was already too late. Montgomery had struck first. The German front west of Caen was in flames.

*

The full weight of the Epsom attack fell on the German front on 26th June. There had, however, been a preliminary attack on the 25th. It was carried out by the 49th West Riding Division of the British XXX Corps. It was the task of this corps to protect O'Connor's troops on the western flank. That western flank had been worrying General O'Connor. His advancing infantry and tanks would be moving across the gunsights of German panzers on the higher ground of the Rauray ridge. That is why, on the day before Epsom, the 49th West Riding Division of XXX Corps was sent forward with supporting tanks to capture it.

What has gone down in history as the battle of Fontenay, started in a thick blanket of morning mist. Five hundred guns tore through the muffled, dawn silence. The infantry rose up and moved forward. Vision was down to five yards. The supporting tanks soon gave up. The infantry slogged on and became hopelessly lost. When the sun eventually broke through to reveal patches of blue sky, it was found that the key village of Fontenay le Pesnel had not been attacked. The main objective, the Rauray ridge, lay behind it. It was almost midday when British tanks arrived. The artillery barrage was repeated. It took all afternoon to reach the battered line of the village street. This was the cornerstone of the 12th SS Hitler Youth front and the boundary with the Panzer Lehr Division further west. When night fell, a part of the

(*Left:*) General of the Waffen SS Paul Hausser in the turret of a Mark IV panzer. (*Right*) Men of the 9th SS Hohenstaufen Panzer Division moving across Europe by train towards Normandy.

village was still in German hands. Over four hundred men had been killed and wounded, half from a battalion of the Royal Scots, and half from the 3rd Battalion of the Hitler Youth Grenadiers.

The Panzer Lehr Division, further west, had, however, collapsed. The 49th West Riding Division had broken through and had outflanked Fontenay. Rauray was under threat from the west. Panther tanks of the Hitler Youth Division had crossed into the Panzer Lehr area to counter-attack and hold the British advance at Tessel Wood.

The telephone line between the 12th SS Hitler Youth and the I SS Panzer Corps buzzed with argument and counter-argument until past midnight. General of the Waffen SS Dietrich wanted the Hitler Youth to withdraw all its panzers from defensive positions and concentrate them overnight for a continuation of the counter-attack on the Panzer Lehr front. SS Standartenfuehrer Kurt Meyer of the Hitler Youth Division was protesting that this would seriously weaken his defences at a time when British troop movements were building up in front of him. The British might attack at any time. Dietrich was sympathetic, but there was just no reserve, and a dangerous gap had opened up. He would have sent the Corps Tiger tank battalion, but that would not get there in time. The argument finished with a compromise. Meyer would withdraw and send west only the 5th and 7th Companies. The

Fontenay-le-Pesnel. In the foreground is an abandoned German anti-tank gun; a panzer grenadier lies dead on the road, and two knocked-out tanks can be seen in the distance. The one on the right is a Panther.

Panther battalion was already there and the 6th Company was in the middle of the battle at Fontenay. The other two companies he would keep in defence.

Nightfall had brought mist over the low-lying ground. It started to drizzle. The few Hitler Youth grenadiers left in Fontenay abandoned their piles of rubble and moved back to dig in on the Rauray road. A platoon of 12th SS Engineers moved into St Nicholas farm. Mark IVs of the 5th and 7th Companies moved out of their defensive positions and crunched their way slowly through the drizzle and darkness towards Rauray.

The British front was alive with movement, too. Long files of Scottish infantrymen were squelching through the wet and dark night to reach their assembly areas. They would attack at daylight.

And, there where the sharp end was at its sharpest, sentries in little holes in the ground were fighting what was always their toughest battle, the fight to stay awake. Drops of rain dripped from their helmets. They wiped wet faces and blinked nervously into the night. Huddled mates lay slumped at the bottom of narrow trenches, sound asleep, oblivious of the danger, oblivious of the water trickling down inside tunic collars, and dead to the whispering silence of the gently falling rain.

49 WEST RIDING DIV

12 SS 'HY' Pz DIV

CHAPTER FOUR

Scotland the Brave

26th June 1944

> ... to the good company, platoon or section leader, who carries forward his men or holds his post and often falls unknown. It is these men who in the end do most to win wars.
>
> *Wavell*[7]

'Ask him who he thinks is going to carry him if he's wounded!'

The padre was always pulling Sergeant Blair's leg about his fifteen stone. But it was Sergeant Walker, who passed the padre's message on, whose body would have to be carried from the battlefield – dead.

Dawn had opened its eyes on lowering clouds and misty fields bustling with men. Country roads had turned into mud. Little Norman villages were alive with jeeps, carriers and lorries: Norrey-en-Bessin, Putot-en-Bessin, Secqueville and Bretteville l'Orgueilleuse – Bretteville the proud? What, one wondered, was the story behind that?

Scotland the brave stood around in the morning mist, tense with nervous excitement, schoolboy wit and foolish grins as camouflage cream was smeared over white faces. Rifles and machine-guns were being cleaned and oiled; rations were being stuffed into small packs; corned beef, cheese and hard biscuits. Cigarettes and boiled sweets were carefully counted and handed round.

'Is General Montgomery nae here to hold our hands then?'

'Ye'll nae find the likes o' him here, Jimmy.'

'But didna he say he'd march wi' us hand in hand?'

The minutes raced by. With this weather there would be no bombing support from the RAF. H-hour approached. Silence fell. All were listening.

0730 hours: A vicious crack flashed from a hedge nearby, followed immediately by a great thunder of distant gunfire. Through it all cut the vicious pang-pang-pang of the nearby field guns. The earth trembled. The noise went on and on. Death went hurtling through the sky above, a shrill whistle faint above the din. It made the skin ripple hot and cold. Men looked over, one to the other, startled, bemused, and they shouted to make themselves heard.

The barrage moved forward one hundred yards every three minutes. It was falling on a front only two miles wide. Seven hundred Scotsmen, the first thin line of assault troops, rose from the sodden and flattened corn. Deafened by the noise, a last fag still hanging from the lips, they walked into the mist and disappeared in the billowing dust and smoke thrown up by the barrage. Clanking slowly forward with them were the supporting Churchill tanks.

For Sergeant Jimmy Blair of the 2nd Glasgow Highlanders it was battle for the first time; a first experience of the fear and excitement, and of the sense of isolation and loneliness, too.

> We soon bumped into a burst of machine-gun fire. The enemy positions were well camouflaged. My friend Walker was killed... Others were killed by snipers . . . they didn't attempt to take cover, walked on forward instead of dropping down and crawling . . . showing their heads above the corn, looking for the enemy... We reached a hedge. Lying there wounded was the company commander and my platoon leader. Another officer lay dead nearby.
>
> As I pushed on there were shouts of 'Get down! – Get Down!' Each time we passed, one by one, through the hedge, there was the crack of a sniper's bullet. But we were quick. Nobody was hit. We advanced in little rushes, firing at where we thought the snipers were. Two came out, hands in the air. I was angry at the thought of my dead and wounded comrades. I felt like doing them in then and there. But we sent them back.[8]

The crews of a German mortar platoon had sheltered from the artillery barrage in their deep bunker. When they emerged to man their firing positions they found they were already surrounded by furious Scotsmen throwing grenades. The following account comes from one of those taken prisoner:

> Pelzmann, fifty yards farther on in the camouflaged observation post, was still fighting. In a semi-circle in front of his camouflaged position were many dead British soldiers. Suddenly the concealed top of the observation post was opened and out came Pelzmann. Holding his sniper's rifle by the barrel he broke the stock against a tree. He

then called out loudly: 'No more ammunition! I've killed enough of you – now you can kill me!' A big red-haired *Engländer* went up to him, seized him by the collar, and shot him through the temple with his revolver.[9]*

It was eleven o'clock in the morning when the Glasgow Highlanders reached the first lateral road, the road that ran from Caen westwards through Fontenay le Pesnel. Sergeant Blair had just sixteen men left of the thirty he had started with: 'But we were flushed with success. We pushed on towards Cheux.'

The 9th Cameronians advanced from the village of le Mesnil Patry. Hardly had they left the start line than they were in trouble. The Churchill tanks that were to support them ran into minefields on both sides of the village. Some lay stranded with broken tracks; all were halted. There they were stuck until the mines could be lifted. The infantrymen pushed on alone. An error on the maps took them right into the path of the British artillery barrage. Men of the right-hand company were dropping, killed or wounded, amongst them all the officers except one. The bodies were hidden in the growing corn. To prevent the tanks running over them, comrades thrust rifles bayonet first into the ground and hung a steel helmet on top, making them look 'like strange fungi sprouting up haphazardly' in the corn.

The advance continued in a confusion of dust, noise and smoke. It seemed to take a long time to get to the halfway mark, the lateral road running between Caen and Fontenay. There they overran some German positions; but there had been heavy losses. Many junior leaders had been killed. Quarter of an hour had been allowed for reorganisation, but the Cameronians needed more than that. 'A' Company was so under strength that it had to be replaced by 'C'. There was still no sign of the tank support catching up. When the Cameronians finally got going again it was without the advantage of the artillery barrage. That had already moved on without them.

The Scotsmen were now through the thin main line of the enemy defence; but so well had many of the positions been camouflaged, that they had passed by without seeing them. The Hitler Youth grenadiers were coming to life in the rear of the assaulting infantry. Troops overrun are usually so demoralised that they give themselves up. Not so with these young Hitler Youth soldiers. They were shooting up the British troops following in the rear. 'Snipers!' was the warning on

* Oberscharfuehrer Ernst Behrens, 12th SS Engineers.

every tongue. These were no snipers, just ordinary infantrymen who were fighting on after their positions had been overrun.

Following as reserve battalion on the right flank was Lieutenant Robert Woollcombe with the 6th King's Own Scottish Borderers. He was sent out with a patrol to search the recent field of battle:

> Suddenly we froze at a burst of fire from Black's Bren gun, firing from his hip, and instantly an apparition rose screaming from the corn and rushed towards us, throwing itself at my feet. . . By a neat bit of shooting Black had hit him, and his left shoulder was streaming with blood. He knelt at my feet, clutching my knees, frantic with pain and terror. 'Don't shoot – don't shoot! Have pity! Don't shoot!. . .' For a few speechless seconds we gazed at him. Black alone stood apart, a little upside down, surveying the results of his handiwork.[4]

Prisoners expected to be shot, and many of the wounded refused to allow British medical orderlies and doctors to treat them in any way.

In the middle of the morning a sudden rain-storm drenched the battlefield. It fell on the dead and the wounded; and on the soldiers pushing through the dripping corn, crouching in the sodden undergrowth, searching for an enemy that was maddeningly elusive.

The Scots Fusiliers were in trouble in St Manvieu. Two company commanders were amongst the many killed. It was a nest of enemy strongpoints. It was also the headquarters of the 1/26th Battalion Hitler Youth Grenadiers. The King's Own Scottish Borderers were sent to help.

The village church tower could be seen amongst the trees a mile away. There were flashes of bright flame and puffs of black smoke. Flame-throwing tanks* were burning out the defenders. The rain was still pouring down. The Borderers sloshed through the dripping corn and arrived at the first shattered farms. Some had been strongpoints with trench systems linking deep bunkers. Three dead Fusiliers lay on their backs staring upwards. Houses were burning, smoke drifted about. Flaming roof timbers were collapsing in a flurry of sparks. Rubble had fallen across the streets. Blackened walls showed where flame throwers had spewed out their liquid fire. The artillery barrage had passed on. Suspense was creeping through the litter of gardens and outhouses. Silence was listening to the crackle of burning wood and the whip and

* Flame-throwing Churchills (Crocodiles) from 79th Armd Div.

'Silence fell. All were listening.' A Scottish infantryman awaiting the signal to advance.

Scottish infantry advancing on St Manvieu supported by Churchill tanks.

A Sherman tank of the 23rd Hussars awaiting the order for 11th Armoured Division to advance. In the background is St Manvieu, where the Scots Fusiliers are in battle.

Scottish infantry in St Manvieu.

whistle of an occasional stray bullet. Lieutenant Woollcombe stumbled on the remnants of one company of the Scots Fusiliers:

> A number of dulled men in steel helmets wearing anti-gas capes against the rain were discovered in a captured German position: Scots Fusiliers, twenty-eight of them, and all that was left of a company that had crossed the start-line that morning. The company commander was dead and a tired captain with handle-bar moustaches was in command. . . He had been reduced to a state of fatalism and recited to me their losses in a strain of mournful satisfaction. . .[4]

Isolated strongpoints of the Hitler Youth were still holding out. A flame-throwing Churchill tank waddled forward, to halt, hissing and smoking, in the park entrance to the German headquarters. It kept breathing out its thin red tongue of flame, sending back clouds billowing upwards, leaving bushes and grass on fire. It blew up suddenly, with a great bang and vivid flash of light. It had proved to be the true harbinger of another world for both friend and foe.

This was the one part of the front where 12th SS still had a panzer company in support. With all communications cut, with his forward company already overrun, the battalion commander was desperate. Only a panzer counter-attack could save them. Off went a runner with the message to the farm at la Byude, a mile and a half away. He drew fire as he ran across the Fontenay–Caen road. Tommy was everywhere. Just beyond, the SS battalion medical aid post was hurriedly loading the wounded into an ambulance, packing up, making a getaway whilst there was still a chance. At Byude he passed on his breathless message.

It brought a disappointing answer from the panzer commander. '*Geht nicht*! – To attack amongst buildings without infantry is not on! Street-fighting is no place for panzers without infantry protection.'

That was a lesson that some of the tanks of 11th Armoured Division would learn before the day was out.

During the afternoon there were still pockets of resistance holding out in the village, but St Manvieu had been lost, and the main battalion headquarters at Château la Mare was moving out too. There the battle had caught up with the French civilians. Mademoiselle Morel was the owner:

> Artillery fire of unbelievable violence descended on us. The maid

(*Left*) SS Standartenfuehrer Kurt Meyer (Panzermeyer). commander of the Hitler Youth Division.

(*Below*) (l to r) General of the Waffen SS Sepp Dietrich, commander of the I SS Panzer Corps, and Field-Marshal Gerd von Rundstedt, German Commander in Chief in the West.

was calling in the cows through a hole in the wall. Eleven of them were caught in shell fire and killed. At midday our shelter received a direct hit and was destroyed. Then the stables were set on fire, killing fifteen of the horses.[8]

Madame Guillaume, in the next farm, had taken refuge in the cellar. She could hear the SS coming and going above her. Machine-guns were firing not far away. The SS were packing up, moving out in a hurry before the Tommies arrived. She went to the cellar aperture and looked into the courtyard. They were gathering there, and as they moved off, they looked down, and it seemed to her that it would not have needed much to provoke them into opening fire.

It was not long before khaki figures came cautiously around the corner into the farmyard. Madame Guillaume, a Belgian national, caught sight of the lion of Scotland shoulder flash, and mistook it for the lion rampant of Belgium. She rushed out to throw her arms round the neck of the nearest Jock and overwhelm him with a flood of Belgian kisses.

Meanwhile, on the western side of the advance, the Glasgow Highlanders had reached Cheux. It was a heap of ruins in a sea of churned-up mud and rainwater. Little battles were going on everywhere. The rear elements and artillerymen of the Hitler Youth were fighting with the same fierce determination as their infantrymen who had been overrun and left behind.

The Cameronians were also beginning to arrive. They were a good thousand yards east of their objective, le Haut du Bosq, and had not realised it. This little village, the headquarters of the 26th SS Grenadier Regiment, was being left uncleared on the western flank of the British advance. It was going to prove a trouble spot indeed.

*

Before first light that morning, Standartenfuehrer Kurt Meyer, commander of the Hitler Youth Division, had gone to Rauray to watch his panzers counter-attack to help his neighbour. Then suddenly at 0730, all hell had broken loose. Meyer had had to fling himself into the nearest ditch. A massive artillery barrage was falling on the Hitler Youth front. The British were attacking. And just when the front had been weakened by removing the panzers from their carefully chosen defensive positions. Well! Dietrich of the 1 SS Panzer Corps had been warned. Now it had happened.

Meyer sent for his panzer commander, SS Obersturmfuehrer (Lieutenant-Colonel) Wuensche.

> Counter-attack cancelled! Rauray is the key to the defence. Hold it at all costs. Return the Mark IV panzers to their prepared defensive positions north-west and south-west of Cheux.

Kurt Meyer raced back to his headquarters at Verson. The following message had just arrived from the 12th SS Engineer Battalion, holding the front north of Cheux.

> All anti-tank guns destroyed – battalion overrun by British tanks – trying to smash through to our bunker – defensive positions in and around Cheux still holding – what about a counter-attack from Rau...[10]

The line had been cut. The British were on the brink of breakthrough. Meyer got through on the telephone to the I SS Panzer Corps. The front was collapsing. The 12th SS must have immediate help. This was a crisis!

*

Dempsey, commander of the British Second Army, smart in his raincoat and red-banded hat, was on his way to O'Connor's headquarters. He felt reassured. He had just read this extract from Field-Marshal Rommel's weekly report: 'In England another sixty-seven major formations are standing to, of which fifty-seven at the very least can be employed for a large scale operation.'[11]

The deception was still working. German intelligence was still reporting a non-existent American army poised at Dover for a second invasion. But how long would it be possible to keep all those divisions of the German Fifteenth Army standing inactive in the Pas de Calais, just two days' march from Normandy?

He found O'Connor with plenty to think about. The advance was running behind schedule. The German front had been more thinly held than anticipated but German positions were springing to life after the assault waves had moved on. Casualties had been heavy, and even after an advance of almost three miles the Scotsmen were not out into the open. Indeed, opposition at Cheux had brought them to a halt. Time was passing. If the tanks of 11th Armoured Division were to have any hope of getting to Hill 112 before dark they would have to

(*Above*) The first German prisoners. 'hands held half-heartedly aloft, some wounded . . .'

(*Right*) Major-General 'Pip' Roberts, commander of 11th Armoured Division.

go soon. It might mean they would have to fight a way out of the end of the Scottish corridor. It was at best only two miles wide, and it ran at right angles across the existing road system. If the tanks failed to get out into the open, with more space to manoeuvre, there would assuredly be a traffic snarl-up. Should Major-General MacMillan of the 15th Scottish now send in the three battalions of infantry he was holding in reserve, or should 'Pip' Roberts and his four hundred tanks be launched and left to fight their own way into the undefended enemy rear.

Major-General 'Pip' Roberts had been a captain of tanks at the beginning of the war. No one in the British Army had experienced so much battle in the turret of a tank. He had fought with the Desert Rats through the north African campaigns, and had now, at thirty-seven, become the Army's youngest divisional commander.

After the Scottish attack had gone in that morning, Roberts had moved his tanks forward to pre-arranged forming-up places on the battlefield. They had moved through the minefields. They had passed the immobilised Churchill tanks, and the crews, who were waving and laughing; free, with that sensation of release soldiers have when 'their' battle is over.

They came to a German trench and German dead. There were British bodies, too, and another tank, still burning. Then across the fields towards them came the first German prisoners: a handful of helmetless and dirty and tired youths in heavily stained camouflage smocks, hands held half-heartedly aloft, some wounded, and behind them a Scottish infantryman, bayonet fixed. Germans! The first that these tank men had seen. Morale went up. Wide fields of rain-soaked corn stretched away into the distance. There were no roads here. The advance would have to be across country. 11th Armoured Division had already suffered its first tank casualty. The Sherman of General 'Pip' Roberts had run over a mine and lost a track. He had commandeered another. Lieutenant Steel Brownlie was a tank commander with the Fife and Forfar Yeomanry:

> The time had come to disperse and await the order to advance. There was a steady drizzle which had soaked everybody to the skin. A few shells dropped close, and we ducked for the first time. We took the spare cans of petrol we had been carrying, and filled up.

The tank men waited and watched. Shells screeched past overhead, and they could hear the steady rumble of artillery fire falling on the battlefield in front of them. Columns of black smoke were rising up, and there was the distant sound of machine-guns. Ambulances were coming back, and a few small groups of walking wounded came trickling past.

15 SCOTTISH DIV

CHAPTER FIVE

The Tank Battle

26th June 1944

' "A" Squadron of the Northamptonshire Yeomanry will advance through Cheux and seize the crossings of the Odon at Tourmauville and Gavrus.'

It was ten minutes to one when the order arrived. The Northamptonshire Yeomanry was the reconnaissance regiment of 11th Armoured Division. Instead of the usual armoured cars, they had Cromwell tanks. 'It was thought,' said General 'Pip' Roberts, 'that being tanks they would have a better chance of breaking out. I never thought much of their luck if they had to make a fight of it.'

Cheux was a shattered chaos of confusing battle. It raged everywhere: amongst the houses, in the orchards and woods, and along the debris-piled streets. This was no battalion battle. Little groups of men led by junior officers, NCOs and private soldiers were fighting it out with similar groups of the enemy. Shells and mortar bombs were falling, and each flat explosion brought a reflexive jerk from soldiers creeping through the debris and sloshing through the mud and water. Flames were licking broken walls and eating their way across the gables, smoke drifted skywards from burning vehicles.

The Cromwell tanks of the Northamptonshires kicked and reared over the litter-strewn, shelled-holed streets; they crashed past falling walls. Tank commanders were standing, with head poking out of the turret top; only in that way could they see to find a way through this confusion of battle. They were sniped at; they used their revolvers to shoot at determined Hitler Youth grenadiers who had jumped on to their tanks to fix magnetic mines. It was two o'clock when they finally shook themselves free of the village. Half an hour later they were on top of the high ground, ring contour 100, just to the south.

Here they were engaged in a tank duel with the panzers (Mark IVs) that had been sent back from Rauray to take up their old positions south-west of Cheux. The German tank commander has given this account of the battle :

> Even as we were moving across [from Rauray] we could see many enemy tanks on the higher group on our left. Before we had reached our old positions under cover of a hedge, a panzer duel had started. As British tanks had already broken through at Cheux we made a fighting withdrawal southwards across two or three fields surrounded by hedges. There were successes and losses on both sides. Crossing my path, a few metres away, Sergeant Buchholz, who was standing in the turret, had his head torn off by a direct hit.[9]*

One troop of Cromwells under Lieutenant Stock managed to find a way through to the railway at Grainville, where they shot up a surprised group of 20 mm flak guns. The others failed to get through. Two were destroyed, four men were killed, three were missing and two had been wounded. The remaining Cromwells were withdrawn.

O'Connor had ordered the tank regiments of 11th Armoured to push forward and take the lead. The fire power of three tank battalions should get them through. It seemed that a collapse of the enemy defence must come soon. Midday had passed and time was running out.

By this time the brigade of Churchill tanks supporting the Scottish infantry had also emerged south of Cheux. They pushed forward on to the high ground just abandoned by the Northamptonshires. Spandau fire bounced off the steel hulls right and left, but it was only when the leading Churchill poked its turret over the crest to get a view that a solid high-velocity shell whipped by just overhead. The German panzers on the other side had that skyline in their sights.

> Lieutenant Barrett's tank was then knocked out . . . he himself, along with Lance-Corporal Cairns and Corporal Murray, was killed. Shortly afterwards Captain Webb's tank was hit on the turret by HE, blinding both him and his gunner.[12]†

Lieutenant Brownlie was with the tanks of 11th Armoured Division as they moved towards Cheux. The Fife and Forfar Yeomanry were on the exposed flank facing Rauray. Their orders were to pass through Cheux and move on south-west through le Haut du Bosq to Grainville.

* Untersturmfuehrer Willi Kaendler, 5th Company, 12th SS Panzer Regiment.

† Major Joscelyne – 7th Royal Tank Regiment (31st Tank Bde).

From there they were to push south to seize the bridge over the Odon at Gavrus before moving on to the high ground beyond.

> At last the order came over the air to move. We had gone about three hundred yards when two armour-piercing shots came through us from somewhere on the right, sending up showers of earth and killing a couple of infantrymen on the ground. We wheeled right and picked up the turrets of three Tigers at about 1,800 yards' range. After an exchange of shots for some minutes they disappeared. They had destroyed a halftrack belonging to another unit. We passed on. I lost my troop sergeant, Greenfield, through engine trouble.

The Fife and Forfars had been fired on not by Tigers but by Mark IVs of the Hitler Youth Panzer Regiment. They had hurried across from Rauray, hoping to occupy their old positions north-west of Cheux. They were too late. While 'C' Squadron drove straight for the village of Cheux, Brownlie, with 'A' Squadron, tried to by-pass it on the left:

> Deep sunken lanes and ditches barred the way. We then tried to get round on the right. Don Hall took his troop round the edge of a wood. There was a terrific flash, a roar, and his leading tank dissolved in a cloud of smoke and flame. The second tank went up an instant later. Don himself came roaring back round the corner, laying smoke. I took cover at the edge of the wood. Where was the fire coming from? What with the trees and smoke I could see nothing to fire at. Two shots whistled past overhead. Two burning, shrieking figures appeared, running towards me, clothing blazing, one quite unrecognisable. I pointed the way they should go.

Trooper Ron Cox was a wireless operator with the squadron that went into Cheux:

> It was the first utterly destroyed village I had ever seen. We moved along a lane leading towards le Haut du Bosq. We were in single file with my troop leading. Our tank was the fourth from the front. We were the Firefly with the more powerful seventeen-pounder gun.
>
> We edged slowly forward and, suddenly, at the top of the lane, where it bends and loses the protection of the high embankments, Corporal Goddard's tank was hit. It did not brew up. Arthur Goddard, a Cockney regular soldier, and his gunner, Lance-Corporal James Low, were both killed. Reagen, the driver, and Vaughan got

'O'Connor had ordered the tank regiments of 11th Armoured Division to push forward and take the lead.'

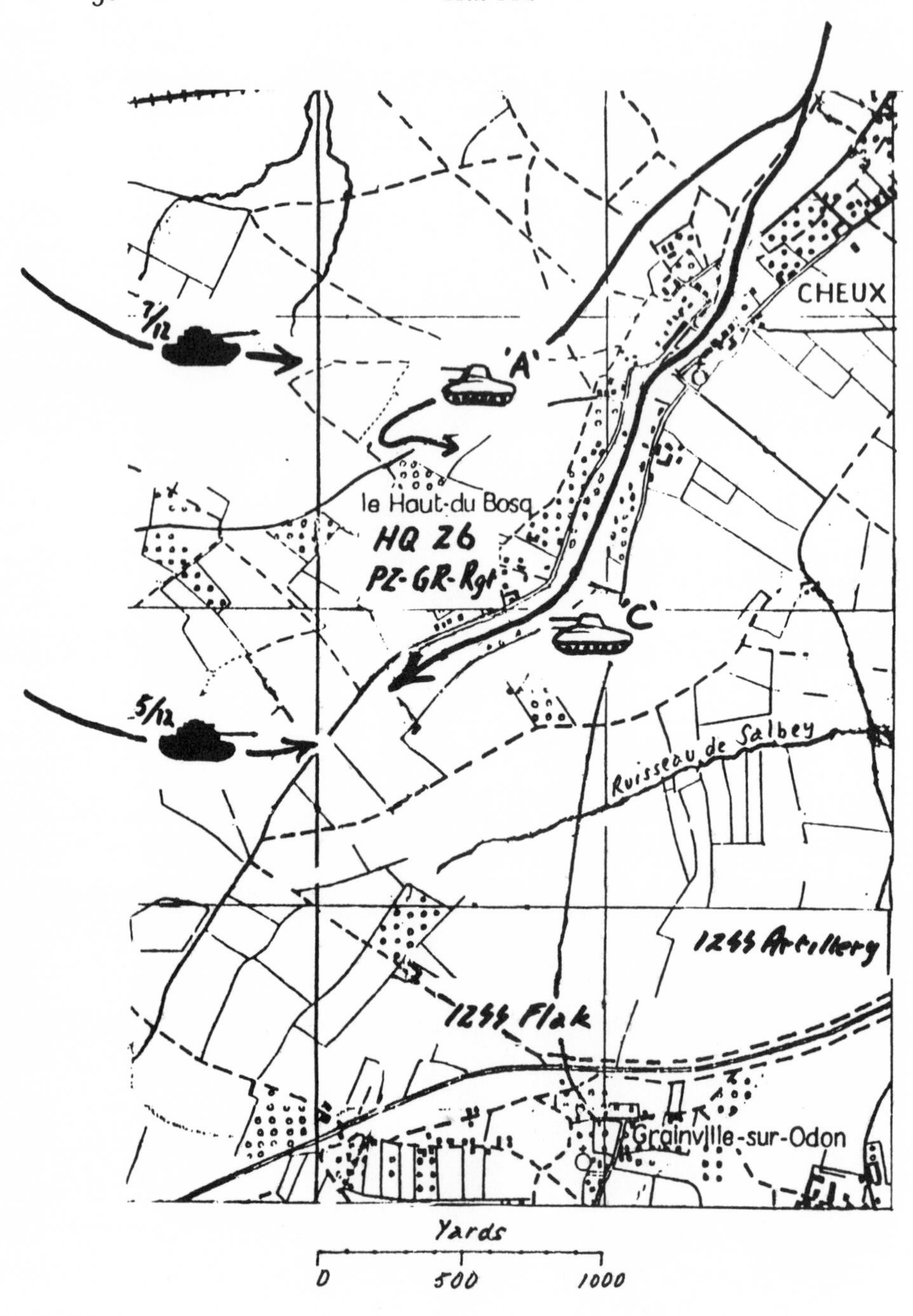
CHEUX
7/12
'A'
le Haut-du Bosq
HQ 26
PZ-GR-Rgt
'C'
5/12
Ruisseau de Salbey
12SS Artillery
12SS Flak
Grainville-sur-Odon
Yards
0
500
1000

> out.* Sergeant Stewart's tank then pushed forward but it, too, was hit. The crew baled out; two had been wounded. A German gun or tank had its sights lined up to shoot anything that emerged. We couldn't go forward, neither could we move right or left. Hemmed in between steep banks we could see nothing. There was no room to turn round, and we couldn't reverse because of the tanks lined up nose to tail behind us.
>
> We had to sit there, trapped and inactive, while all around us the battle raged. Messages were being passed over the air without any attempt at security. We heard the commanding officer, Lieutenant Colonel Scott, frequently coming on the air urging the squadron leader to advance. But Major Nicholls had had considerable experience of battle in the desert and he retorted that he would advance only when the gain justified the losses. That was a great morale booster to us. We were surprised to hear him say that to a superior with us listening in! But we knew that under Nicholls we would not be sacrificed needlessly.†

These Fife and Forfar tanks had been brought to a halt by the Mark IV panzers that had rushed back from Rauray to go into defence on both sides of the road, watching the exit from the village. They had arrived in time to plug the gap.

*

During the afternoon, the 12th SS Hitler Youth Division received this message of help from 1 SS Panzer Corps:

> One company of the Tiger panzer battalion now moving towards Grainville. One panzer and one assault-gun company of 21st Panzer Division will move into area Verson and come under your command.

Army Group 'B' had come through with the promise of two infantry battalions of the 1st SS Adolf Hitler Panzer Division, but these were still some distance away. The 7th Mortar Brigade had also been ordered into the crisis area. But the problem was an immediate one. British tanks and infantry were through at Cheux, threatening to overrun the 12th SS artillery. Only the German artillerymen, some headquarter troops,

* Goddard's name is on the Bayeux memorial to those with no known grave. Low is buried nearby in Fontenay le Pesnel.

† Nicholls, wounded on 18 July, went off to help some of his crew who had been trapped, and was never seen again.

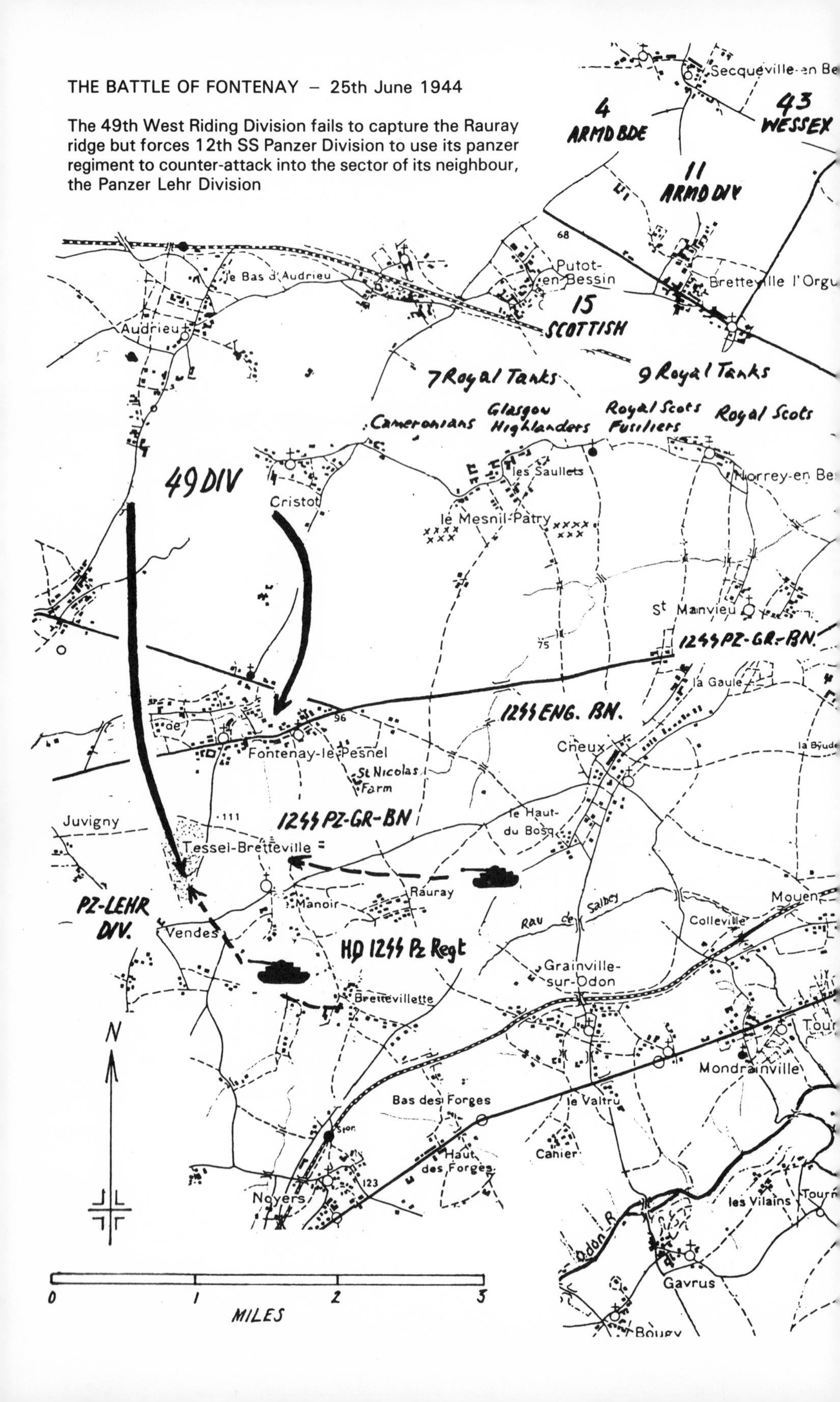
THE BATTLE OF FONTENAY – 25th June 1944
The 49th West Riding Division fails to capture the Rauray ridge but forces 12th SS Panzer Division to use its panzer regiment to counter-attack into the sector of its neighbour, the Panzer Lehr Division
4 ARMD BDE
43 WESSEX
11 ARMD DIV
15 SCOTTISH
7 Royal Tanks
9 Royal Tanks
Cameronians
Glasgow Highlanders
Royal Scots Fusiliers
Royal Scots
49 DIV
12SS PZ-GR-BN.
12SS ENG. BN.
12SS PZ-GR-BN
PZ-LEHR DIV.
HQ 12SS Pz Regt
Secqueville-en Be
Putot-en-Bessin
Bretteville l'Orgu
le Bas d'Audrieu
Audrieu
les Saullets
Norrey-en Be
Cristot
le Mesnil-Patry
St Manvieu
la Gaule
Fontenay-le-Pesnel
St Nicolas Farm
Cheux
la Byude
Juvigny
le Haut-du Bosq
Tessel-Bretteville
Rauray
Manoir
Mouen
Rau de Salbey
Colleville
Vendes
Grainville-sur-Odon
Bretteville
Tour
Mondrainville
Bas des Forges
le Valtru
Cahier
Haut des Forges
Noyers
les Vilains
Tourn
Odon R.
Gavrus
Bougy
N
0 1 2 3
MILES

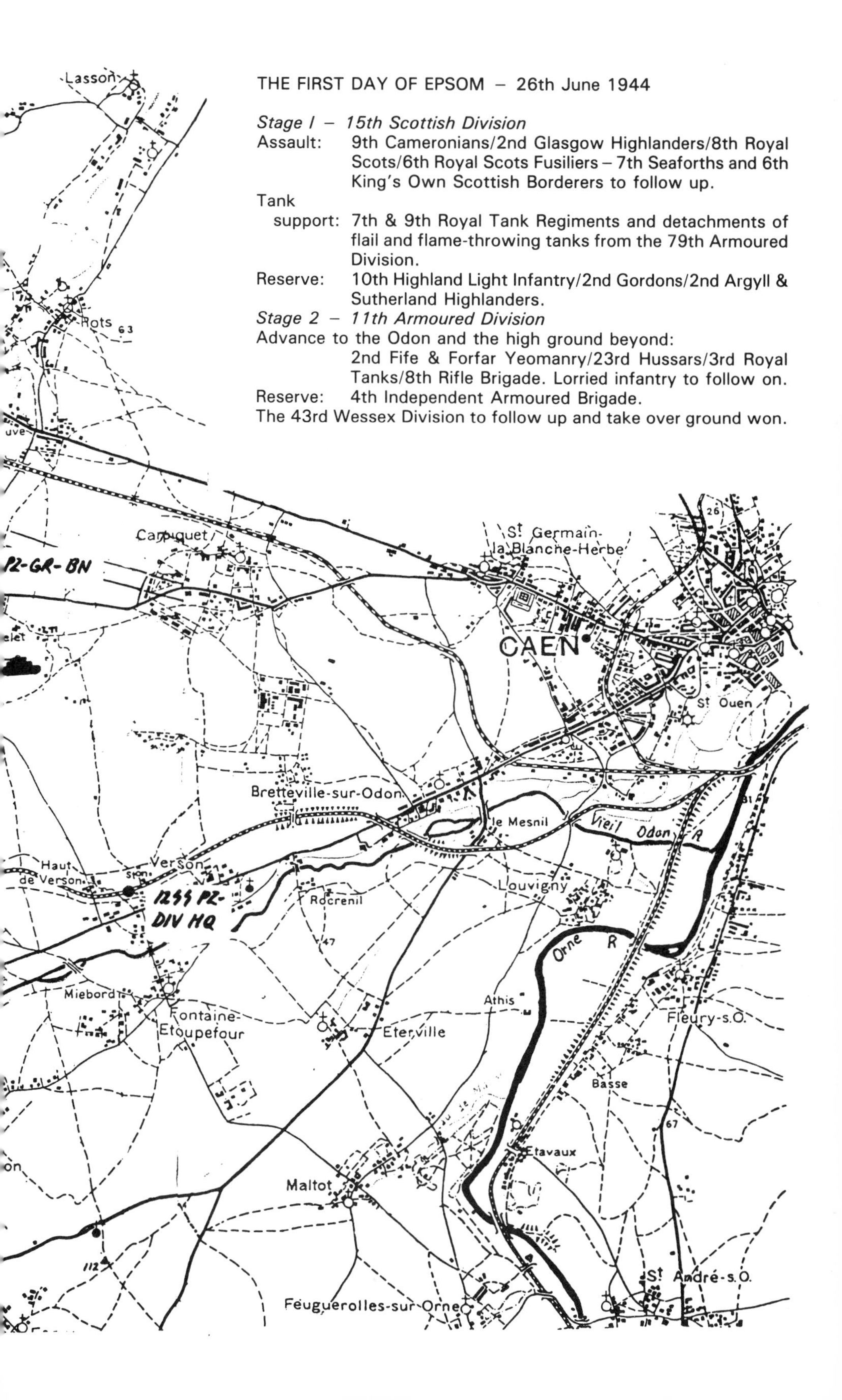
THE FIRST DAY OF EPSOM – 26th June 1944
Stage I – 15th Scottish Division
Assault: 9th Cameronians/2nd Glasgow Highlanders/8th Royal Scots/6th Royal Scots Fusiliers – 7th Seaforths and 6th King's Own Scottish Borderers to follow up.
Tank support: 7th & 9th Royal Tank Regiments and detachments of flail and flame-throwing tanks from the 79th Armoured Division.
Reserve: 10th Highland Light Infantry/2nd Gordons/2nd Argyll & Sutherland Highlanders.
Stage 2 – 11th Armoured Division
Advance to the Odon and the high ground beyond:
2nd Fife & Forfar Yeomanry/23rd Hussars/3rd Royal Tanks/8th Rifle Brigade. Lorried infantry to follow on.
Reserve: 4th Independent Armoured Brigade.
The 43rd Wessex Division to follow up and take over ground won.
Lasson
Rots
63
Carpiquet
PZ-GR-BN
St Germain-la Blanche-Herbe
26
CAEN
St Ouen
Bretteville-sur-Odon
le Mesnil
Vieil Odon R
Haut de Verson
Verson
Stn
12SS PZ-DIV HQ
Rocrenil
47
Louvigny
Orne R
Miebord
Fontaine-Etoupefour
Eterville
Athis
Fleury-s.O.
Basse
67
Etavaux
Maltot
112
St André-s.O.
Feuguerolles-sur-Orne

infantry straggling back from positions already overrrun, and a company of recce troops hastily sent forward to plug the gap, were barring the route south to the bridge over the Odon.

The 23rd Hussars had been given the task of fighting a way forward to the Tourmauville bridge. They by-passed St Manvieu, where the battle was still raging, and bogged down in a countryside of thick hedges, sunken lanes and tiny fields surrounded by embankments. It was late in the afternoon when a company emerged south of Cheux. Working with the Hussars were the two companies of the division's motorised infantry, the 8th Rifle Brigade. One company led by Major Noel Bell pushed through Cheux :

> Buildings were in ruins, some still burning. Infantry were still clearing the houses; shooting was going on in another part of the town. In the middle of the road was a dead cow, and near it was a knocked out halftrack. Two men were sitting in the back, huddled forward. Both were dead.

The Seaforth Highlanders could be seen on the high ground just south of Cheux. They were trying to move south towards Colleville and were meeting stiff opposition. The Churchill tanks supporting them were making no progress; three of them were in flames, sending out great clouds of black smoke.

The first Sherman of the 23rd Hussars to nose its way up the gentle slope burst into a ball of flame before the horrified eyes of those following :

> One moment an impregnable monster with a crew containing some of one's best friends, forging irresistibly towards the enemy, the next, a crack of terrific impact, a sheet of flame – and then, where there had been a tank, nothing but a roaring inferno. The driver, Lance-Corporal Hogg, was killed, but the remainder of the crew got out, two of them badly burnt. They hid in the corn, which was now just ripening, and made their way back later under cover of darkness. Shortly afterwards Lieutenant King's tank was hit and knocked out. The rest of the squadron began to move up. Captain Walter went forward to see what had happened, and an armour-piercing shot went through the rear idler of his tank. . . The squadron leader's tank was also hit and immobilized.[1]

Troops of the armoured reconnaissance battalion of the Hitler Youth had been holding this route to the Tourmauville bridge over the Odon, but now a Tiger tank of the 101 SS Heavy Tank Battalion had arrived

Right) 'It soon sorted things ut – brought those probing hermans to a halt!'

Tiger tank of the 101 SS leavy Tank Battalion (I SS anzer Corps).

Below Left) Sergeant Jimmy lair, 2nd Battalion Glasgow lighlanders.

Below right) Sturmmann ochen Leykauf, 12th SS litler Youth Reconnaissance attalion.

and was picking off the British tanks. In the words of Kurt Meyer of 12th SS: 'It soon sorted things out – brought those probing Shermans to a halt!'[10]

Grey-black clouds, heavy with rain, had thrown the battlefield into premature darkness. Suddenly they broke. Water came down in torrents. It soaked the infantrymen to the skin; it poured down in steady streams on the crewmen in their leaky tanks; and it added to the misfortunes of Sturmmann (Private) Jochen Leykauff of the Hitler Youth Reconnaissance Battalion. He had lost touch with his comrades as they drew back before the British advance:

> I pulled myself under the bushes. Three little tracked vehicles came rattling past, white five-pointed stars painted on the side. The rain was pouring down. I crawled back further. A camouflage smock. Someone groaning softly. I pulled him carefully under the bushes. My hand was covered with blood. I tried to get his first-aid dressing out. I pulled up the smock and uniform jacket. The bullet had come out close to the kidneys. 'Water' he muttered. I took off my helmet and put it in the rain. The enemy tanks were getting closer. . . One broke through the hedge just in front of us. We couldn't stay there. I told him that I was going to look for a better place. I made a dash for it. A machine-gun burst, just above me. I pressed myself into a furrow. Then I made another dash. Again the machine-gun fire. It hit the ground all round me. Something told me this was the end. The firing seemed to come from above. A tank machine-gun. Close to, on the right, a shout through the rain: 'Hands up!' I pressed myself still flatter. Another burst. . . Once again: 'Hands up!' A motor started up. There was the sound of tracks.
>
> Then I saw the tank, on the right. Someone in the turret was looking across at me. I stood up slowly, and knew that this was the end. The man in the turret waved me to the rear. I had the feeling that he was going to shoot me in the back. I walked up to the tank, looked up into his eyes and said in English: 'A wounded comrade lies in the bushes over there!' The wireless was chattering away through the sound of the motor. A tank port opened up in front of me. Out jumped a man. He drew a revolver. 'Do you take prisoners?' I asked. He made a gesture with the barrel. I undid my equipment. He was not going to shoot. I just stood there: 'My comrade?' He pushed me away with the revolver. I walked away. And I felt ashamed.[9]*

* Sturmmann Jochen Leykauff, 12 SS Reconnaissance Battalion.

The attempt of 11th Armoured Division to fight a way through to the high ground beyond the river Odon had come to an end. The 23rd Hussars had been unable to get over the crest just south of Cheux, and the Fife and Forfar tanks were still halted in le Haut du Bosq. They were in difficulties, for the rear end of the squadron column had come under attack. Five more Shermans have been knocked out, four more crewmen killed, and three more wounded. 'We stood,' said Ron Cox, 'with heads just above or below the turrets, with grenades in our hands, equally ready, I think, to throw them or surrender.'

Had the Fife and Forfars had the 11th Armoured infantry with them they would not have been trapped in this way and would have had every chance of fighting their way forward. The British experience of tank warfare came from the battles in the wide open spaces of the desert, where tanks manoeuvred like ships on a sea of sand, doing their own thing. Normandy was different. It was a maze of winding country roads, of tall embankments, of clusters of farmhouses, of woods and copses and orchards. Here it was easy to destroy tank mobility, to trap tanks, to leave them at the mercy of both long-range and short-range anti-tank missiles. The British were learning the hard way, that only by working closely together would tanks and infantry be able to make progress.

Four Scottish infantry battalions had been in the forefront of the advance. They had fought themselves to a standstill. Half their fighting men had disappeared, and most of them would reappear only on the casualty lists. Many of the young officers, the sergeants and corporals and those natural leaders in the ranks that battle always brings to the front, were no longer there. 'Straightway all the best men died,' wrote Homer many centuries ago. In that respect war had not changed.

General Macmillan of the 15th Scottish had, however, kept three battalions in reserve. He now sent these fresh troops forward with orders to take over the advance and get through to the river before nightfall.

The 10th Highland Light Infantry advanced on the right, passed through Cheux, and started to move south along the road to Grainville. They didn't get far. Bullets whipped past in the pouring rain, and the men dropped to cover in the sodden grass. 'We dug in for the night under intermittent mortar fire. To add to our wretchedness, the rain still persisted, although we were already so wet that we scarcely heeded the downpour. . .'[13] *

* Sergeant Green, 10th HLI.

The 2nd Gordon Highlanders took over on the left. They were to move through Cheux, and push on over the high ground to Colleville down in the dip beyond.

Even before the storm that evening Cheux had been a muddy snarl-up of tanks, ambulances, Bren carriers and other army vehicles. The cloud-burst had flooded the streets of rubble and debris to form great pools of muddy water in the low-lying spots. The only route south was through Cheux. Converging on that battered village, where German snipers were still active, were the transport and troops of the Highland Light Infantry, the Seaforths, the Cameronians, the Glasgow Highlanders, and their supporting Churchills from the Royal Tank Regiment, together with those of 11th Armoured Division.

The two forward companies of the Gordons had managed to push through quickly. They had advanced through the rain, over the high ground and had disappeared beyond the crest. When battalion headquarters emerged from the chaos of Cheux these two companies had gone. They were out of wireless contact. No runner had come back. What had happened to them?

Artillery forward observation with the Gordons was Captain Mike Peppiatt:

> My first action – the roar of hundreds of guns – shell-scarred Cheux a military Piccadilly Circus – the rain, fierce, relentless, soaking us to the skin. Down a sunken lane. Some of our wounded there, tended by a medical officer and a padre. There was a lot of blood.

Captain Peppiatt was given orders by the commanding officer of the battalion. Two companies were believed to have got through to Colleville. Wireless contact had been lost. He must get through with the Bren carrier to help them.

> I'm soaked through. A quick swig of whisky – that's better! We go down the lane in the carrier. A dead cow blocks the track, and we drive right over it. . . Round the bend. . . Soldiers – three of them – in field grey! This is definitely not 'A' Company. Turn round; must get out of here quickly. That dead cow again. More soldiers – ten, fifteen, twenty – all in grey uniform! I fire at them with my revolver. An explosion! The carrier lurches, sways, jerks to a stop. We're surrounded. The driver's head is bleeding.

Captain Peppiatt and the carrier crew were taken prisoner. His carrier

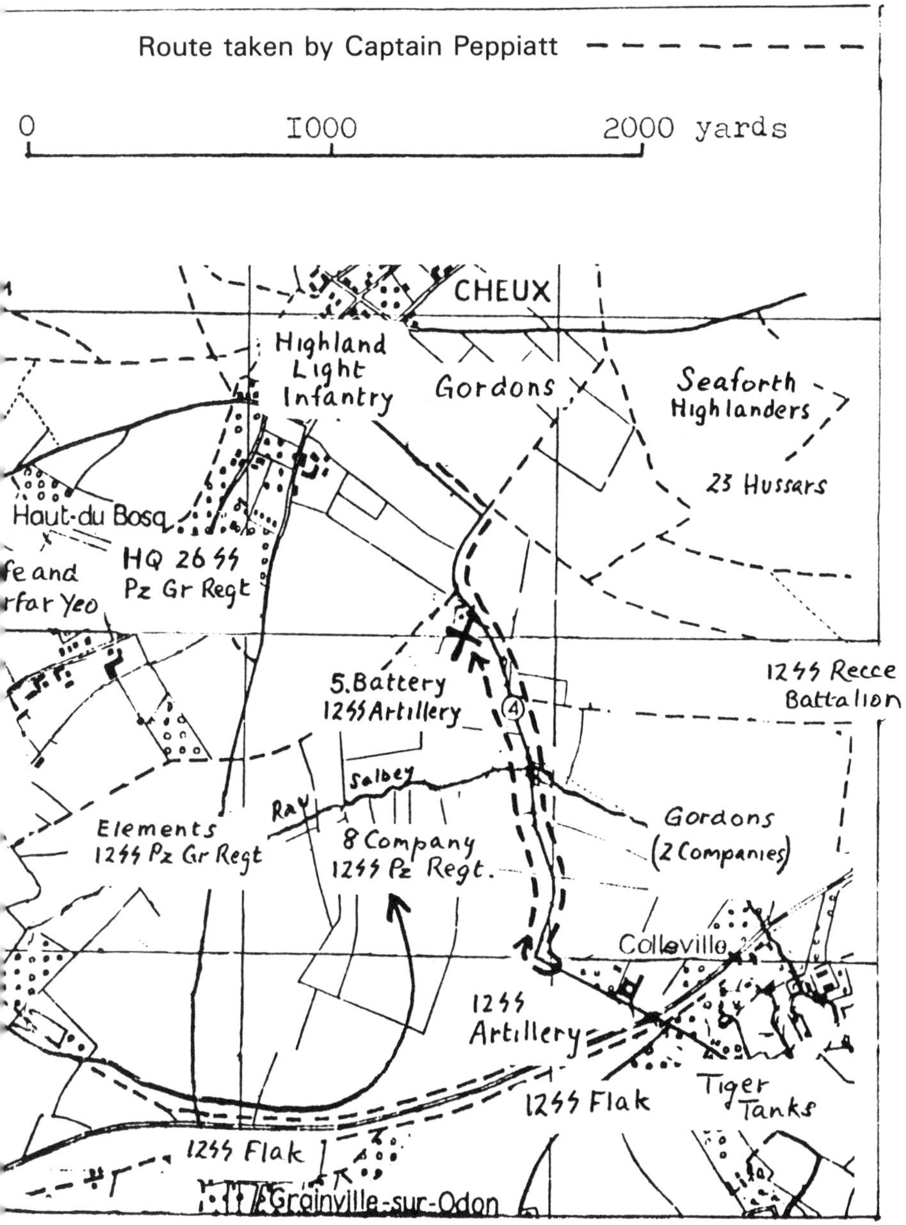

Route taken by Captain Peppiatt - - - - - - - -

0 1000 2000 yards

CHEUX

Highland Light Infantry

Gordons

Seaforth Highlanders

23 Hussars

Haut-du Bosq

HQ 26 SS Pz Gr Regt

fe and rfar Yeo

12 SS Recce Battalion

5.Battery 12SS Artillery

Salbey

Rau

Elements 12SS Pz Gr Regt

8 Company 12SS Pz Regt.

Gordons (2 Companies)

Colleville

12SS Artillery

12SS Flak

Tiger Tanks

12SS Flak

Grainville-sur-Odon

had run into the gun positions of the 5th Battery of the Hitler Youth Artillery Regiment.

The German battery commander had gone into Cheux and failed to return. The gun-towing vehicles had been destroyed by artillery fire. Communications had broken down. Oberscharführer (Sergeant) Hans Hartmann had seen Peppiatt's carrier go past. Suddenly it came back along the track:

> I let it come to within ten yards and clearly recognised it. I fired a panzerfaust. It hit but did not explode. I jumped out of the way. It rattled past artilleryman Domes, who was lying in the ditch with another panzerfaust. He fired it into the rear at a range of about five yards. It hit the left track. A captain and three men were taken prisoner. Fifteen minutes later I heard another vehicle approaching. This time my panzerfaust hit and exploded, and Domes hit it also. It was another British carrier. A British officer and the driver were killed; a third man we took prisoner. I sent them all back to my headquarters. Major Schoeps came to see us and said he would send a panzer as soon as it got dark to pull the guns back.[16]

Captain Peppiatt, Royal Artillery, and Captain Wishart of the Gordons, for that was the name of the officer killed in the clash with the second carrier, failed to return, and nothing more was heard that night of the two companies of Gordons that had pushed on in the direction of Colleville.

Cheux remained a bottleneck. It was past midnight when the medical officer of the 23rd Hussars at last got through to attend to the wounded.

Lieutenant Steel Brownlie spent the last hour of daylight in the wood on the northern edge of le Haut du Bosq, where he had earlier taken cover:

> I was firing and being fired at by panzers further west. But the light was bad and the range so great that I could not be sure of results. When the order to harbour was given, I found it an almost impossible task in the darkness and confusion to find the rest of the squadron. It took an hour to get to them, creeping about in the blackness, lit up only by flaming wrecks scattered everywhere. I found that, in spite of the horror of the night, Sergeant Greenfield was in a state of elation. He had got his tank going again, and had gone on straight into the village [le Haut du Bosq] where 'C' Squadron were held up

> and surrounded and had lost some of their tanks. He had done a lot to clear things up by using his Browning machine-gun mounted on the turret. 'C' Squadron got out as it was getting dark, and thought themselves lucky, for the Germans were in that part of the village.

Trooper Ron Cox takes up the story :

> Inch by inch we edged backwards down the very long lane, back into Cheux village. A big barn was on fire, and men were dashing about in the light of the flames trying to put it out with buckets of water. 'C' Squadron had lost seven of its nineteen tanks; ten tank crew had been killed and five wounded.

Darkness and exhaustion brought an end to this first day of Epsom. All the formations that had been in direct contact with the enemy had been fighting their first battle. They had been pitted against Germany's finest troops, the Waffen SS, all of whom were volunteers, young men deeply committed politically, of high morale, and led by officers and NCOs of proven courage and wide experience. Four battalions of Scottish infantry had borne the main burden of battle. They had attacked with great spirit, and had paid for their successes with ninety percent of the casualties suffered by VIII Corps.

The British had failed to achieve their objectives, the crossings of the Odon and the high ground beyond. But they had broken into the German defence and thrown the German front into confusion. They were well placed to continue the advance the next day.

The VIII Corps war diary stresses the close country that helped the defenders, who had had time to prepare; that most of the fighting had been at close range, with the enemy sitting tight in thick cover until he had every hope of a 'kill' with the first round or burst of small arms fire. Two officers and one hundred and sixteen other ranks had been taken prisoner : most were from the Hitler Youth Engineer Battalion, but two were from the Panzer Lehr Division.

*

The 12th SS Hitler Youth was hanging on south of Cheux with that grim tenacity that made the Waffen SS such formidable opponents. At St Manvieu they had mounted a counter-attack with the help of panzers from the 21st Panzer Division, only to see it nailed down by a deluge of

British artillery fire. 'If reinforcements are not sent tonight, nothing will prevent a British breakthrough tomorrow!'[14*]

This cry for help to General Dollmann of the German Seventh Army shows the extent of the crisis. The reply only serves to emphasise it:

> No reinforcements available. 1st SS stranded at St Germain [a hundred miles away] without petrol. It will be two days before new infantry divisions arrive.[14]

It was suggested that help should be sought from the 2nd (Vienna) Panzer Division, which was holding the front west of the Panzer Lehr Division.

General Dollmann was worried enough to get through to Field-Marshal Rommel at ten o'clock that evening:

> The situation is very grave. I propose that the II SS Panzer Corps counter-attack immediately.[14]

Rommel agreed that on no account could the British be allowed to encircle 12th SS and 21st Panzer Division:

> Everything that can be assembled must be thrown in; but II SS Panzer Corps is not yet complete. 2nd and 21st Panzer must each send a tank battalion, 2nd SS a battlegroup, and the 7th and 8th Mortar Brigades must be sent in support.[14]

The I SS Panzer Corps battle headquarters, in the village of Baron, had come under heavy British shellfire. About midnight it informed Kurt Meyer of 12th SS that it was moving back about two miles. It was pointed out that the 12th SS headquarters in Verson was dangerously exposed and should also be moved. Meyer replied that to pull the headquarters back would be bad for morale. The hard-pressed troops must feel that the division had confidence in the outcome of the battle.

*

The headquarters of the 1st/26th Battalion SS Panzer Grenadiers, which had held out in St Manvieu all day, moved in the night to Marcelet, taking with them some wounded and some prisoners.

* Based on extracts from the Seventh Army Telephone Log for 26th June.

The headquarters of the 12th SS Engineer Battalion, a solidly constructed bunker just south of the Caen–Fontenay road, was overrun by the Glasgow Highlanders, who did not stop to examine it. The bunker was then attacked by a British tank, which fired into it with its seventy-five millimetre cannon, killing two of the occupants and wounding others. But the tank, too, moved on. Several times grenades were tossed into the bunker, and there was one determined attempt to get the occupants to surrender. When night fell, however, the battalion commander and a handful of his men were still there, and, as before, the British had lost interest and moved away. At midnight, leaving two badly wounded men behind, the remaining seven men left the bunker and moved south through the black night. It was pouring with rain. Halting frequently to let the wounded catch up, they skirted the British tank harbours and gun lines. The only dark figure to confront them turned out to be one of the Hitler Youth sergeants, who was also trying to get back south. The light of dawn made further progress impossible. They hid, wet and exhausted, in a ditch, and fell into a deep sleep.*

Also moving south through the rain that night was Captain Peppiatt, prisoner of the Hitler Youth. They were in the valley of the Odon when the German column halted and he was taken into a house. He had been looking for an opportunity to escape in the dark :

> Now there are only four Boche and four prisoners. We are very hungry and the sausage and black bread are welcome. Sleep on the floor... Are they asleep? No-one is on guard. I'm too tired... Sleep...

*

Just before nightfall, Haupsturmfuehrer (Captain) Siegel had arrived south of Cheux with the last four panzers (Mark IVs) of his company. He had been ordered to block the route to Colleville and pull out the Hitler Youth guns for Major Schoeps.

Sergeant Hans Hartmann's battery was pulled back to the crossroads south of Grainville, and he was ordered to wait there with the gun crews; transport, said Major Schoeps, would come and pull them further back in the morning.

But Major Schoeps would not survive the night to arrange that. He was with Siegel and his panzers near the Salbey stream, and about to move off in his Volkswagen, when a Scottish fighting patrol sprang silently out of the rain and darkness. In the hand-to-hand tussle for life

* They were found by German tanks that counter-attacked later in the morning.

and death that followed, Schoeps was badly wounded and bled to death.

Lieutenant Steel Brownlie, back behind Cheux with his tank in harbour, had time to reflect on the sobering experiences of the day. Lieutenant Pritchard was missing, Sergeants Christie and Hulton, Corporal Goddard and Lance-Corporal Low, and Trooper Pirie were dead – the latter on his twentieth birthday :

> We had gained little and lost much. What with the darkness, the rain, the sights we had seen, the tension and fear, and the three hour wait for the petrol and ammunition to arrive, even the hardy Sergeant Greenfield sat awake all night; hardly an eye closed. We were only a few hundred yards from the enemy, and the worst fear of any tankman is to be attacked in harbour at night.

'The cloud-burst had flooded the streets . . . Note the direction sign with the name 'Schöps', the artillery commander who was killed in a clash with a Scottish night patrol.

Lieutenant Robert Woollcombe was in the village of St Manvieu:

> The rain dripped and trickled into our trenches, and there had been no hot food since dawn. The big shells banging away on the T-roads jarred us, while the faces of the three dead 'Fusiliers' could still be seen there as pale blobs through the gloom and rain, motionless among the shells, with their ghastly whiteness.[4]

About midnight men of the 43rd Wessex Division arrived to take over in St Manvieu. Scotland squelched out in a trance of half sleep, long files of boots heavy with sticky mud, helmets dripping, gas capes flapping against wet legs. They would march the night away before stopping just north of Cheux in a new grey and damp dawn.

Five miles away at Fontaine-Henry and Cainet the infantry of 11th Armoured Division, well back from the front, had spent a trying day with tempers and nerves a little on edge. They had been waiting since dawn for the call that was to take them into the battle. 'Half an hour to move!' had been the warning at midday. But darkness and the rain had come, and the men were still standing around in little groups, lorries lined up, ready to move off.

> Between the showers of rain we watched the reflection of the gunfire on the lowering clouds. The horizon quivered as a thousand eerie spasms of light shot across the night sky. 'That's where we have to go,' said someone. The breath came a little quicker, the heart bumped a little stronger. We knew that our tanks had gone into action during the afternoon. We were learning that battle consists of long periods of waiting. Then came the stand-down order: 'No move before first light!' We went back to our wet slit trenches and crouched there in the rain, waiting for tomorrow. The artillery thundered away. It was difficult to sleep.*

* JJH. 3rd Monmouths (11th Armoured Division).

11 ARMOURED DIV

CHAPTER SIX

Across the Odon

27th June 1944

> That mass of British tanks was enough to frighten anyone to death. There was no time to think any more. Only one thing mattered: to keep fighting! [10]

That is how the battle had appeared to SS Standartenfuehrer Kurt Meyer, commander of the 12th SS Hitler Youth Panzer Division. By the next day, however, Rommel's Army Group 'B' was able to record in its war diary 'a complete defensive success' adding the rider that it had been achieved only by the I SS Panzer Corps 'employing its last reserves'.* But it was a success teetering on the edge of disaster. The telephone log of the German Seventh Army shows that the I SS Panzer Corps was clamouring for help. If reinforcements failed to arrive that night, then there would be a British breakthrough the next day. General Dollmann issued this situation report:

> The enemy – the British 11th Armoured Division – is pushing forward over the Villers Bocage–Caen road and is approaching the Odon river. It has penetrated deeply into the left sector of the 12th SS Hitler Youth Panzer Division, and clearly has the intention of seizing the dominating high ground of Hill 112. [15]

That night troops were on the move towards the threatened area. A battlegroup from the 2nd SS Das Reich Panzer Division newly arrived on the American sector from the south of France, left St Lô just after midnight to report to the 2nd (Vienna) Panzer Division for orders for a counter-attack. The 2nd Panzer Division was to throw in a panzer battalion of its own for this thrust into the western flank of the British

* Army Group 'B' gives the tank strength of the I SS Panzer Corps on 26th June as: 114 Panthers and 200 Mark IVs fit for action. To this must be added the 101 SS Heavy Bn. with eighteen Tiger tanks fit for action.

advance. Infantry and panzers of the 21st Panzer Division were moving from east of Caen to help both Panzer Lehr and the 12th SS Hitler Youth. Two regiments of 88 mm flak guns were moving into anti-tank positions in the Hill 112 area. The advance guard of the 8th Multiple Mortar Brigade was hurrying north to give fire support. The 1st SS Adolf Hitler Panzer Division, still some distance away, was ordered to send on ahead two of its grenadier battalions.

Meanwhile, holding the two routes south, from le Haut du Bosq and Cheux, the defence was thin indeed. Hidden amongst the trees of the Salbey stream valley were the four remaining panzers of Hauptsturmfuehrer (Captain) Hans Siegel. His men had been busy all night pulling the guns of the Hitler Youth to safety. The British night patrol that had killed the artillery commander Schoeps had showed how vulnerable he was on the right. Now that the guns had gone, there was a gap between his panzers and some Hitler Youth armoured cars holding the railway crossing at Colleville. Before dawn he had walked over to the Grainville road to find out if anyone was on his left. He found panzer grenadiers. All asleep. Exhaustion had taken over. They didn't want to hear his warning of a British attack that must surely come with the dawn: 'We've got some panzers there, they can sort it out!'

Siegel hurried back over the damp grass. It was getting light. The British artillery opened up. They were throwing a heavy artillery barrage along the line of the valley. He found his four panzers on the move – backwards. They had thought he was not coming back, and were trying to get out of the range of the gunfire. Siegel took them back to their old positions. There they were protected to the front by a high embankment, leaving only the turret as a target. They had a clear field of fire to the crest of the hill in front, fifteen hundred yards away. Cheux lay hidden beyond.

There, out of sight, forming up for an attack, was the Highland Light Infantry. It had been a night of heavy rain and little sleep. A dawn breakfast of soya bangers and hard biscuits had done little to raise a warlike spirit. The commanding officer was not happy about the failure of the attack the previous evening. It had been a damp and dismal disaster. Now the battalion had a second chance. The objective was the bridge over the Odon at Gavrus; but first they had to get to Grainville. They moved forward through the early morning mist. The British field guns started up behind them – much closer now, they had moved forward during the night. Suddenly blinding flashes shot through the tops of the trees and there was a loud crash of explosions. They were under fire. All had thrown themselves flat on the ground. Shrapnel sang through the damp air in a whining diminuendo. Branches, twigs and showers of leaves tumbled down.

'Stretcher bearers!' The shout was taken up elsewhere.

Other shouts were heard now. 'On your feet!' – 'Keep going!' – 'Leave the wounded!' They rose up. They moved on. The start line was somewhere ahead.

They moved on up to the crest through the standing corn, and then over the top and into the sights of Captain Siegel's four panzers. There was to be no victory for the Highlanders here.

> Frantically they went to ground, but mercilessly the enemy mortars plastered the cornfield. Training had taught them much, but could never teach the horror of seeing their friends torn to pieces before their eyes.[13*]

Siegel's panzers were firing with their machine-guns only, holding back their cannon fire for the supporting Churchills that were following. As the British tanks came over the crest they opened up. They saw the crews baling out as tanks were hit. Some were burning. The others turned round and disappeared with the retreating infantry behind the crest. The Highland Light Infantry had received a bloody nose. When the reserve companies tried to get the attack moving again they received the same treatment.

The distress of the Highlanders was complete when they found that battalion headquarters was fighting for its life against enemy Panthers that had suddenly appeared in the orchards and amongst the farm buildings behind them. Trucks belonging to the headquarters had been hit and were ablaze. Captain Scott had to swing his anti-tank guns around one hundred and eighty degrees to hold this attack from the rear.

The regimental aid post was caught between two fires. The wounded lay in the shelter of a wall. Solid armour-piercing shot was skimming across the top, chipping off lumps. Stretcher-bearers were crouching below, moving the wounded to a place of greater safety.

Some of the panzers – the Panther battalion of the 2nd (Vienna) Panzer Division – pushed the attack right into Cheux itself, where they surprised and knocked out two reconnaissance tanks (Honeys) belonging to the 23rd Hussars. Sergeant Scott, asleep in one of them, was killed. Lieutenant Brownlie, waiting in his Sherman tank just south of the village, heard the firing and confusion behind him:

* Sergeant Green, 10th HLI.

> Four Panther tanks came into Cheux from the other side. They routed the infantry and got to within two hundred yards of us. I saw one commander blown out of his turret, about twenty feet in the air, before landing back in the inferno that had been his tank.

The men of the Highland Light Infantry, bitter at their casualties and lack of success, were angry when they pulled back and saw Sherman tanks of 11th Armoured Division waiting inactive just south of Cheux. 'When we had needed them most, we had looked in vain for their mobile fire power!' complained one, and another eye-witness spoke of 'lanes filled by our tanks, closed down and deaf to all appeals.'[13*]

These Shermans of the Fife and Forfar Yeomanry were now ordered into the battle. Lieutenant Steel Brownlie moved forward with 'A' Squadron:

> It was up to us to try where the Churchills supporting the Highland Light Infantry had failed. Our flimsy Shermans were not at all suited for such close fighting. To reach the objective, we had to advance up a slope, over the sky-line, and down into the woods in the valley beyond [the valley of the Salbey stream] where the enemy positions were. We advanced two troops up, Freddie Craig on the right, and myself in reserve in his rear. No sooner had he topped the ridge than his three tanks were hit and brewed, while he himself ducked for cover into a slight hollow. I had to come up and take his place, so, sergeant leading, I moved. The 17-pounder Firefly was lagging behind, and in spite of all my efforts on the air it would not come up. The sergeant topped the ridge safely and was racing flat out down the slope when I crossed. A Panther emerged from the woods on his left and fired on him. Unaware of the danger, Sergeant Greenfield kept firing into the green stuff to his front. I fired at the Panther and tried to warn him on the air. Everything went wrong. A shell jammed and the electricity went – radio, gun traverse, engine, intercom., and firing gear. I couldn't move, I couldn't speak, I couldn't fire the big gun, and I was sitting on top of the ridge, looking at the Panther, which was slowly traversing its gun in my direction. Then, with my machine-gun bullets bouncing off it in all directions, the enemy panzer turned and disappeared back into the wood. Greenfield had by this time gone right on into the trees. Later his tank was brewed up there. Thomson and Sykes were killed, Harper died of his wounds, and Greenfield and Martin were badly burned.

* Sergeant Green, 10th HLI.

Brownlie's Sherman was towed back towards Cheux, carrying back Scottish infantrymen found wounded in the standing corn. The tank crew set to work on the edge of the village. Despite the mortar fire that kept sending them to ground, the fault was found and remedied, and Brownlie went into the village :

> I wanted to restock with ammo, so I set off in search of the sergeant major. I found the village strangely deserted, and on turning a corner found myself face to face with a Panther squatting in the middle of the road. I put up enough dust to cover a regiment in retreat.

Panther tanks had also moved into le Haut du Bosq, as the 5th Duke of Cornwall's Light Infantry found out when they arrived expecting to find the Cameronians. The leading company was beginning to dig in at the western end of the village, when they heard a roar of engines and clank of tracks. The menacing black crosses on the turrets of the tanks that then appeared came as a shock. Four British anti-tank guns moving unsuspectingly along the village street clashed head on with them and were destroyed and left burning with frightening ease. Four Panthers broke through a hedge and rolled into the field where company headquarters was digging in. For the infantrymen it was a rapid exit to the nearest cover. By this time two battalion six-pounder anti-tank guns had unlimbered and had started firing. One of the Panthers burst into flames. The battalion commander arrived in the middle of the confusion and uncertainty. One of the guns was smashed by a direct hit. Lieutenant-Colonel Atherton had replaced a wounded crewman on the other. That gun, too was hit and put out of action. Two German motorcyclists came driving along the village street and were shot and killed. The shout for PIATs* had brought four teams into action. One Panther, hit and damaged, disappeared out of the village the way it had come in. Sergeant Hicks and Corporal Ronan knocked out a second, and two more clanked their way into the sights of Private Blackwell's PIAT. One was knocked out, the other turned over in a ditch as it was trying to get away.

In this, their first battle in World War Two, the 5th Duke of Cornwall's Light Infantry had destroyed five Panther tanks. Nine German crewmen had been killed, four had been taken prisoner. They

* PIAT – Projectile Infantry Anti-Tank. The British equivalent of the German panzerfaust. It was clumsy, inaccurate and less effective, but it was put to good use here.

had themselves lost twenty men in killed and wounded: amongst the dead was their battalion commander, Lieutenant-Colonel Atherton.

The German Panthers, without infantry protection, were just as vulnerable as had been the Shermans of the Fife and Forfars in this same village the evening before. The new hollow charge, hand-held infantry anti-tank weapons were making it impossible to send in tanks without infantry to keep the enemy infantry away.

It was the I SS Panzer Corps that had ordered this thrust through le Haut du Bosq into the flank of the British advance. Crisis and confusion had set the counter-attack off at half cock.

'Order, counter-order and disorder' is a much used army saying. It had not been the intention to send those Panthers into battle without infantry to protect them. Battlegroup Weidinger (2nd SS) should have been with them: two battalions of infantry and another company of tanks, with mortars and anti-tank guns in support. The I SS Panzer Corps had given the order; the Panzer Lehr Division had countermanded it, diverting Battlegroup Weidinger to plug the gap between them and the Hitler Youth; the Panthers of the 2nd (Vienna) Division had been left with the disorder. They had counter-attacked alone. That they had caused surprise and spread confusion, penetrating right into Cheux itself, shows that had the counter-attack gone in as planned it would assuredly have brought the British advance to a halt and caused a considerable delay.

*

Hauptsturmfuehrer Siegel and his four Mark IVs had repelled each successive British attack from their almost impregnable positions in the Salbey valley. But about midday Siegel's luck ran out. In order to get a better view of his dangerous right flank he moved from his good cover to a position further right. One of the British tanks had pushed on ahead and entered the trees level with him but some six hundred yards away. Branches prevented him from firing, and Siegel's attention was taken by another attack coming in:

> We were firing so fast that the ventilators could hardly cope with the fumes. Then the ground in front of us appeared to explode – a tank shell! The lone enemy tank was now only four hundred yards from us. Before we could swing the gun round he hit us. On the front, the right-hand side. The panzer seemed to explode in flames. The gunner baled out. He was on fire. The loader got out on the other side. I tried to get out of the top of the turret but was held

'One was knocked out, the other turned over in a ditch as it was trying to get away.' Burning Panther destroyed during the counter-attack on 27th June.

A Hitler Youth Mark IV panzer captured intact south of Cheux being towed back through the village by a tank recovery vehicle of 11th Armoured Division. The number on the turret shows that it belonged to Hauptsturmfuehrer Siegel's 8th Company. The 12th SS sign can be seen on the right of the hull.

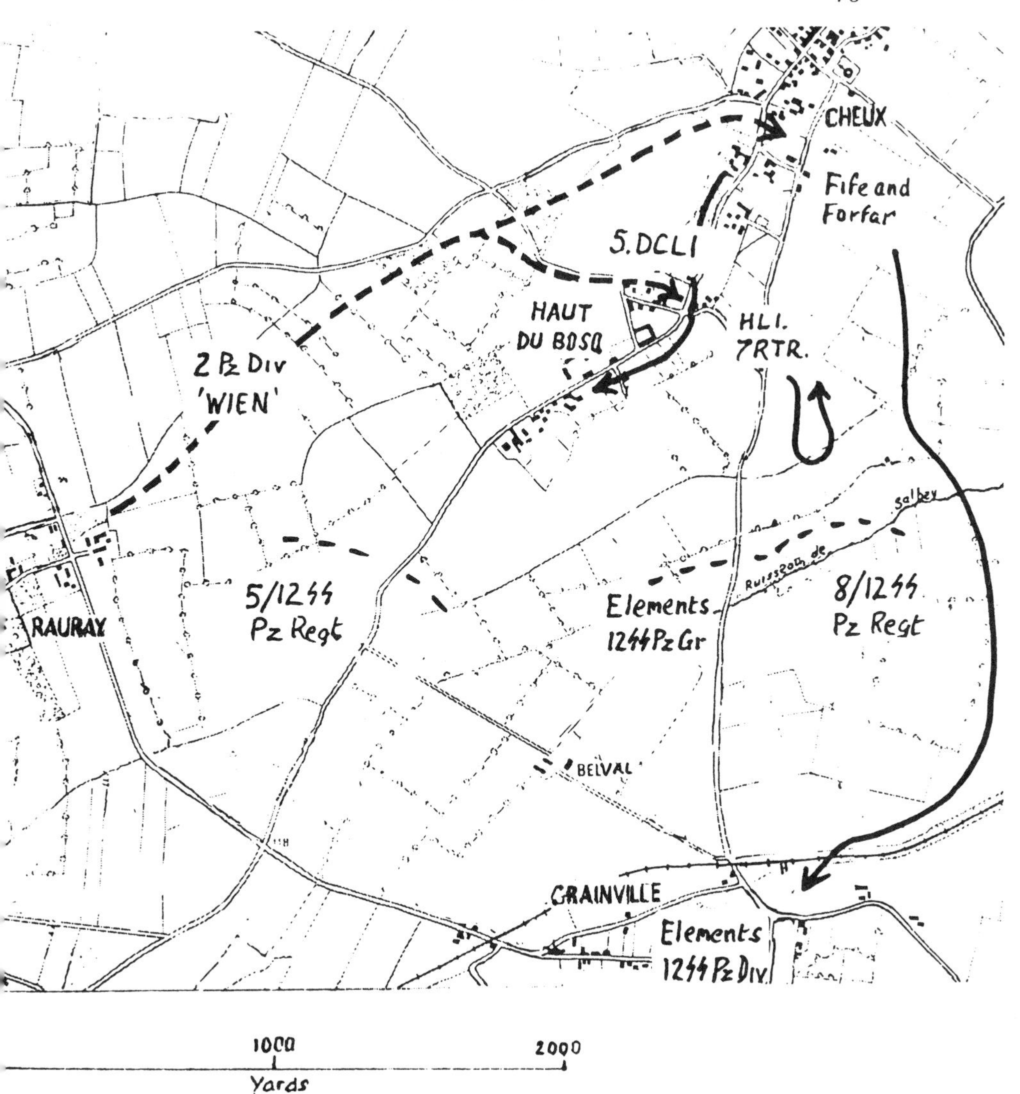

27th June 1944 – Battles in the West
The 2nd (Vienna) Panzer Division counter-attacks out of Rauray with a battalion of Panthers and clashes with the 5th Duke of Cornwall's Light Infantry as they move into le Haut du Bosq.

An advance of the Highland Light Infantry, supported by tanks of the 7th Royal Tank Regiment is thrown back by the 8th Company 12th SS Panzer Regiment and elements of 12th SS Panzer Grenadiers.

In the afternoon the Fife and Forfar Yeomanry fight their way through to the entrance to Grainville, where they are later joined by the 9th Cameronians.

> back by the wire of the neck-microphone. I tried to follow the loader and collided head-on with the wireless operator, who couldn't get his own exit port open. I pushed him through. I was losing consciousness. But I managed to make the jump, only to remain hanging on the side of the panzer, almost strangled, still held by the neck-microphone, which wouldn't go over the helmet. With a mighty tug I broke loose. The driver remained in the panzer; perhaps wounded or killed, for his escape port was open and he would otherwise have got out. The gunner was lying on the ground, still burning. We tried to lie on him to stifle the flames. He wasn't wearing the leather uniform. He died later in hospital.

Siegel and the other two crew members were all severely burned.*

When his squadron returned to refuel, Brownlie was able to rejoin. They advanced once again towards Grainville:

> This time there was no opposition. We crossed the railway line, and from the high ground there I put some high explosive into German camouflaged vehicles far-away to the south. Don Hall and I sat in the shelter of the smoke from a burning house, and watched the light recce tanks under Kenneth Matheson go into Grainville to see if it was clear. One of them was knocked out by a Panther in the church square.

Matheson came roaring back out of Grainville at top speed. It was not the right time for Lieutenant-Colonel Scott to come up on the air with a request for his exact position: 'Position be buggered!' came the reply. Even the colonel had no answer to that.

The Fife and Forfars were not going to make the same mistake as the day before. They were not going to get trapped in the village of Grainville as they had been in le Haut du Bosq. They waited on the outskirts for the Cameronians to arrive. Whilst waiting they sent tanks to probe further west. With them was Trooper Ron Cox:

> Advancing across a large open field, the Sherman of Sergeant Hughie Hutton was hit. Hutton was killed and Andy Freeman had his arm broken; the rest of the crew escaped without injury. The gunner in our tank, Glenn McLeod, a dour man from Gourock, spotted that

* Siegel's account has been published in several books. His panzer was probably knocked out by Sergeant Greenfield of the Fife and Forfar Yeomanry, who had raced ahead and had reached the cover of the trees.

> the shot had come from a shed-like structure. Without waiting for an order he fired and hit it. It exploded, and some of the crew were blown up into overhead wires. In a rage we sprayed them with machine-gun bullets.

The advance to the river Odon had come to a halt on the right-hand axis through Grainville and le Valtru to Gavrus. On the left-hand route to the Tourmauville bridge, two companies of the Gordons had reached the railway line near Colleville the night before. The 15th Scottish now committed a fresh battalion, the only one not in action the previous day, the 2nd Argyll and Sutherland Highlanders. They were ordered to push through the Gordons, cross the main Caen road and seize the Tourmauville bridge with all possible speed.

'The British are here! Don't move!' whispered Monsieur Jean Le Clerc as he crawled back into the shelter at Colleville. After an anxious night he had ventured a few steps outside the shelter. In the farmyard he had caught a glimpse of khaki-clad soldiers. One youth ignored the advice. He had rushed outside, only to rush back, chased by a burst of automatic fire. A period of breathless silence was broken by more bursts of automatic fire. Bullets were hitting the door. Monsieur Le Clerc put a piece of white cloth on a stick and thrust it through the door and waved it. They then all trailed out, one after the other, hands in the air, but not before one British soldier had fired again, killing one of the women.

On the railway crossing north of Colleville were dead and wounded Scotsmen who had walked into the artillery barrage by mistake. The village of Mondrainville was all smoke and explosion. It held the headquarters of the Hitler Youth Reconnaissance Battalion, and there were line of communication troops and a flak battery there, too. A German tank and a group of grenadiers were advancing north towards Colleville. They had been ordered to regain the railway crossing. An eight-wheeled armoured car joined them:

> But Tommy was getting past us on each side to get into the village. We kept firing for all we were worth. The range was short; the effect devastating. Tommy fired smoke back and plastered us with heavy shells. I drove back to the command post in Mondrainville for reinforcements – Flanderka's recce troop. The undergrowth was alive with British infantry. Received a direct hit on one of the wheels. Took over another eight-wheeler that had just arrived. But the British kept

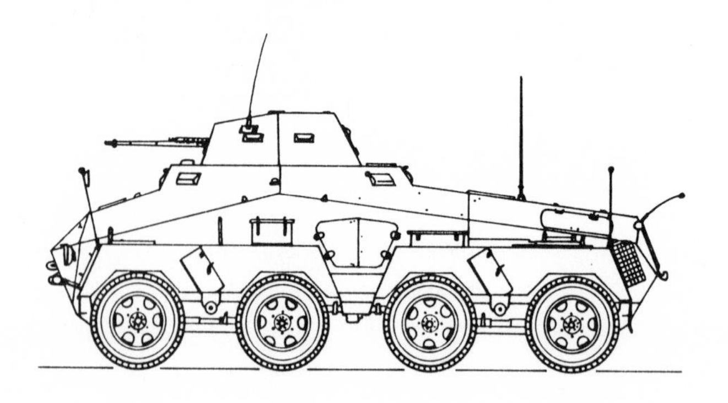

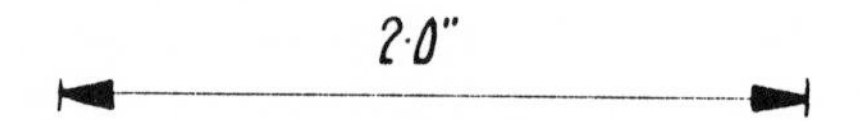

> coming through the hedges. Then they started to fire anti-tank missiles at us. We withdrew back to the main road, firing all the time.*

It was a Canadian lieutenant, Edwards, serving with the Argylls, who was the first to reach the Caen road. He and his platoon were seen by Monsieur Lelarge from his attic window :

> Five or six British soldiers were lying on the road. They had been hit whilst trying to cross. The fire was coming from an apple tree in which a German soldier was hidden. Then a big German tank arrived from the direction of Mouen. It stopped and fired shells in the direction of Cheux. Suddenly it was hidden in thick clouds of black smoke.[8]

The Hitler Youth artillery sergeant, Hans Hartmann, was stranded without transport for his guns, which were on the main road near Grainville. They had been pulled back that far by one of Siegel's panzers during the night. Early in the morning he had gone to the divisional headquarters in Verson for help :

* Oberscharfuehrer (Sergeant) Zinssmeister, 12th SS Reconnaissance Battalion.

> A lieutenant was driving me back along the main road in a Volkswagen. It was a long road, straight as a die. Suddenly British soldiers ran across under cover of smoke, one by one. The lieutenant really stepped on it then. We almost ran into one. When I got back to the guns at Grainville, I found the young artillerymen very anxious and worried. They, too, had seen British soldiers.[16]

By midday panic had seized the many French civilians. *'Il faut partir! – C'est dangereux de rester!'* Prams and carts were loaded with a few precious belongings. News that villagers had been killed by gunfire gave added urgency. Shells and mortar bombs were falling. Telegraph poles were down, wires lay entangled in the road. Sitting around a table in one of the farm gardens were four German soldiers, frozen in that attitude in which they had met death; one had an arm raised with a fork in his hand. On the Colleville turning a British soldier lay dead, his blackened, burnt-out motorcycle in the grass nearby. Houses were on fire. The baker's shop stood, doors wide open, freshly baked bread on the shelves. The Panther was still burning on the main road, its long 88 mm gun pointing in the direction of Cheux, barring the road to further traffic.

Moving south behind the advancing battle front was Sergeant Jimmy Blair of the Glasgow Highlanders :

> We had been north of Cheux, burying the dead. We were suddenly ordered forward. Cheux was full of vehicles again, and the dead of the previous day's battle. I saw two bodies propped half upright in a hedge on the side of the road : one had been literally cut in two. I passed quickly by. Stray bullets were coming past, sending us to ground. We searched the fields of corn, we fired into the trees, not one German did we find. We had just finished digging in near the railway line when we were sent off on patrol. Bursts of machine-gun fire came at us; kept us pinned down for over ten minutes. It was one of our own tanks. They thought we were Germans. Bloody poor shots, if you ask me ![8]

*

The German official who on this morning of confusing battle turned up unannounced at the headquarters of the Hitler Youth Division explained that he had been sent by the German Foreign Ministry. Annoyance at the arrival of this visitor at such a difficult time, turned to incomprehension and then anger when he explained his mission. He had come to find out for the minister why the German army was always retreating. SS Standartenfuehrer Kurt Meyer has described how solid armour-piercing shells were heard smashing into the walls of the headquarters building :

> British tanks were close at hand. The room emptied. The staff had grabbed panzerfausts and were crouching in some hole in the ground outside. I wonder what the messenger of the Foreign Minister made of that? It was the last we saw of him.[10]

*

The tanks of 11th Armoured Division were at first kept out of the battle. Beyond the railway line was country thick with orchards, woods, small fields, tall hedges and narrow country lanes. It was the kind of close country where soldiers pull the trigger first and ask the questions afterwards. The armoured division and the 15th Scottish were separate commands. As we have already seen from the account of Sergeant Jimmy Blair, a clash between British tanks and British infantry could easily arise. But at eleven o'clock the 23rd Hussars began to move forward. Major Noel Bell and a company of the Rifle Brigade in armoured halftracks were moving behind them :

> Some sparks seemed to fly off one of the leading tanks, and the air was filled with a sound like that of a racing car passing at great speed – a rushing, whirring note. A moment's pause and the tank burst into a mass of flames. Micky said : 'Eighty-eights !'* We were too green to be scared. It had not registered on our minds that we must be in the gunner's sights, and that another armour-piercing shell was being loaded into the breech.

The halftracks of the Rifle Brigade swung left to the cover of a farmhouse on the higher ground. They found a light British reconnaissance tank, apparently abandoned, near a high stone wall. 'One of our boys went to investigate, climbed on to the turret and peered inside. He jumped down rather quickly, looking sick.' There was an outburst of firing. One German was killed and two were taken prisoner. Neither looked more than seventeen.

British tanks had reached the railway line at Mouen. Sergeant O'Connell's tank was hit. The crew baled out and had difficulty in

* The 88 mm dual purpose flak gun was much feared by British tank crew. The Tiger also carried an 88 mm gun.

dodging the enemy infantry. Four Shermans were sent on through Mouen to deal with an enemy tank reported there. Only one came back. Major Henri LeGrand, a Belgian officer serving with the 23rd Hussars was one of those who failed to return. His one ambition had been to return to Belgium fighting with a British unit.

Just after midday the tanks of the Hussars emerged from the lanes and orchards on to the main Caen road. The Argylls had already crossed and were pushing towards the valley of the Odon.

Oberscharfuehrer (Sergeant) Zinssmeister was also there with his great eight-wheeled armoured car:

> 'Oberscharfuehrer, is that a German tank?' asked the driver. The gunner fired a dose of armour-piercing shells across its bows, and we were surprised when it disappeared behind a house. We threw the car round the corner, and while I was getting through to report to Flanderka six more Shermans came out on to the road. Armoured halftracks tried to get through to us. One was hit when it tried to turn in the road. It was burning.

Zinssmeister raced off to Grainville, where he found three Panthers. He sent them along the road to halt the British. A message then came over the air; the armoured cars were to report immediately to division at Verson; they were wanted for defence at headquarters.

The 23rd Hussars found Tourville to be 'a wasp's nest only partially smoked out.' The artillery commander of the 15th Scottish, Brigadier Hilton, died of wounds received there in battle with a Panther. Later in the afternoon the Germans satisfied themselves with lining up their sights along the straight stretch of road and taking pot shots at all who tried to cross.

At about five o'clock in the afternoon the Argylls advanced down the sloping fields of corn to dispose of three enemy machine-guns. They moved down the twisting country road to the Tourmauville bridge. No attempt had been made to destroy it.

Half an hour later a dozen Sherman tanks of the Hussars arrived and crossed the little bridge down in the valley, waved on by the Scottish soldiers.

> They ground along in low gear up a steep and twisting track through wooded and difficult country until they came out just south of the village of Tourmauville, where, for the first time, they were able to fan out on ground that gave a good field of fire.[1]

This was the foot of Hill 112. The ground rose in a gradual slope to the crest a mile further on. It was completely open, covered with rough grass, and with a line of hedge and small trees on the summit.

> Commanders and gunners strained their dust-filled eyes. Were some of those bushes camouflaged tanks? One German experienced what was probably the greatest shock in his life. He appeared in a small civilian car from the direction of Esquay. Lance-Corporal Essex put an armour-piercing shot through the car from a range of twenty yards. Surprisingly the driver managed to get out and, though pursued by Corporal Hoggins with a Sten gun, he got away and was last seen going very fast in the direction of Esquay.[1]

Whilst these tanks were exchanging fire with German guns and infantry near the village of Gavrus, other Shermans of the Hussars were involved in battle in Tourville. Two Honey tanks were destroyed. The commanding officer, in a Sherman, came on the air with a plea for help: 'Get behind me, Sixteen Charlie, there's some bugger shooting me up the dock!'

Three anti-aircraft tanks ran into an enemy post; Lieutenant Kerton's Sherman disappeared, the crew was taken prisoner; the intelligence officer and the artillery observation officer both lost their tanks; but by seven o'clock another squadron and headquarters had arrived in the bridgehead. The Sherman tank of the commanding officer lay on its side, overturned on the sharp bend leading down to the bridge. A company of the Rifle Brigade with halftracks and carriers was also across.

The battle raged on all sides. Pillars of black smoke rose skywards from burning vehicles; houses and haystacks were on fire; shells were falling; bursts of machine-gun fire were drowned out by the roar of the heavy cannons of the tanks. A great cloud was hanging over the Odon valley.

Back at Cheux the infantry brigade of 11th Armoured Division was at last arriving to take part in the battle. Sergeant Moppett of the Herefords drove into the chaos of Cheux in his Bren carrier:

> The killed of both sides were lying everywhere. There were abandoned motorcycles and burnt-out trucks, and I counted six of our anti-tank guns, all burning, all still hitched up to their quods.* A

* Gun-towing vehicle.

[T]his German tank knocked-out [o]n the main road at Tourville [is] one of the three Panthers [fr]om the 2nd (Vienna) Panzer [D]ivision sent from Grainville to [tr]y to halt the British advance.

['T]hey moved down the [tw]isting country road to the [To]urmauville bridge.' The [va]lley of the Odon.

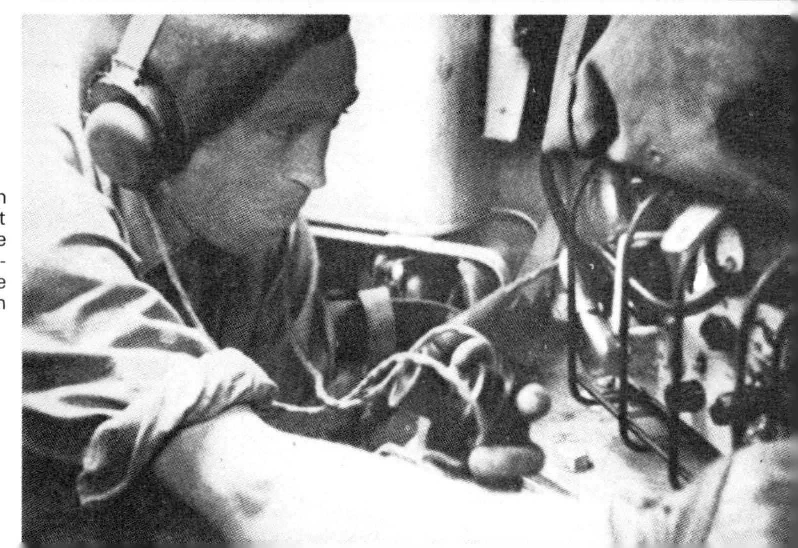

['L]ance-Corporal Essex put an [ar]moured-piercing shot [th]rough the car from a range [of] twenty yards.' Lance-[Co]rporal Essex tuning in the [w]ireless set of a Sherman [ta]nk.

German tank had side-slipped down the embankment and was tilted with its long gun resting on the road. I learned my first battlefield lesson: not to stand up in a Bren carrier. A Churchill tank broke through a hedge and made short work of some snipers in a large house on the left; it put one round of high explosive through each window. We caught up with the battalion on the far side of the village. We waited for orders.

A few hundreds further south, where the country road had steep embankments on each side, a driver was frantically tugging at the wheel of a jeep. The engine raced, the gears crashed. He was trying to turn within the shelter of the embankments. An armour-piercing shell screamed past overhead. A tank duel was being fought out. The sound of battle was all round; the smell of cordite and of the dead hung in the air.

It was here that the brigadier and the three battalion commanders met for the orders group. It was already past eight in the evening, and British infantry and tanks had crossed the Odon more than two hours earlier. No one had told the brigadier that. His orders were to put in an attack south and to get across the river before nightfall. Where was the enemy? No one knew; perhaps in the village of Colleville or Tourville. Where were the British? No one knew exactly.

The brigadier gave his orders: Herefords on the right, Shropshires on the left, Monmouths to stay in Cheux and await developments. Start-line, the main Caen road at Tourville. No time for reconnaissance; no artillery support. The start-line would be crossed at 2130 hours. Any questions? The battalion commander of the Herefords didn't think he could get to the start line on time. The brigadier disagreed. The battalion commander persisted. 'An order is an order!' said the brigadier. 'Carry it out or take the consequences!'

The Shropshires arrived on the main Caen road twenty minutes late. There was no sign of the Herefords. The Shropshires pushed forward alone. The 'attack' became a march down through the difficult country of the Odon valley in single file, a company commander leading with a map. They crossed the Odon on a wooden foot bridge. They moved on, up out of the valley to Baron, where they dug in. They had seen no sign of the enemy; they had seen nothing of the British either. But the Herefords were already there; they had used the Tourmauville bridge and had passed on beyond the tight defence of the Argylls. Major Thornburn, wandering through the darkness in search of them, received a spine-chilling welcome from the most demoralising weapon he ever had to face, the Moaning Minnies: 'If this is war, then it's very nasty indeed!'

*

On the route further west the Gavrus bridge was as far away as ever. The Fife and Forfar tanks waited outside Grainville all the afternoon for the infantry to arrive.

The Sherman tanks were seen by Sergeant Hans Hartmann of the Hitler Youth artillery, who was stranded in Grainville still waiting for transport to pull his four guns to safety:

> I went over to inspect some farmhouses nearby. British tanks were in the orchard. The crews seemed quite unworried, busy amongst themselves and with their weapons. Without thinking of the consequences, I fired at them. They threw everything they had back at me. But I managed to get away, and we loaded one of the guns with solid shot and sited it to cover the road. They didn't come, which was just as well, for we wouldn't have stood a chance. Then an officer and some men of our reconnaissance regiment turned up. 'What are you doing here?' he wanted to know. He ordered us to destroy the guns and go back with him. We hadn't any explosive and by this time bullets were whistling past. So we took the telescopic sights. One of the gunners was hit and killed. We withdrew in stages, firing back as we went.[16]

It was six o'clock in the evening. The 9th Cameronians had arrived with their supporting Churchill tanks. Lieutenant Brownlie watched them from his Sherman tank as they moved into the village:

> They lost a number of tanks and had to withdraw. The infantry caught it especially hard; dozens of them were dragged out in a sorry condition and lay in the shelter of my tank till the jeeps removed them. One poor chap had both his legs blown off. He lay there, his head pillowed on a groundsheet, puffing at a cigarette, apparently quite unaware that both his legs had gone. He died before they could move him.

Panthers of the 2nd (Vienna) Panzer Division had moved into Grainville. Three Churchills were knocked out. A withdrawal was ordered, but the order took a long time to reach the hard-pressed company in

Panzer grenadiers captured in a trench at Grainville.

The howitzers of the Hitler Youth Division abandoned at Grainville.

heavy battle round the church. It was already dark when they withdrew through drifting smoke and the flickering flames of burning houses. They left behind them a din of ear-shattering bangs and crashes, a fireworks display of Very lights, exploding grenades and strings of tracer bullets.

It was midnight. Where there had been uproar and battle there was now the dead silence of darkness. After two days of tough battle the Cameronians had collapsed exhausted into their half-dug slit trenches. The commanding officer, utterly drained by the tension of battle, was asleep in a ditch. The company that had withdrawn with such difficulty from the battle had just discovered that two of their wounded had been left behind. It was the company commander, the medical officer, the padre and four stretcher-bearers who went back to look for them. They wandered through empty and deserted streets. Not a German was to be seen. The Panther tanks that had given them so much trouble by the church were gone. They found the two wounded and brought them back.

The Gavrus bridge was still two miles away.

*

The German command had started the morning with a surge of optimism. General Dollmann of the Seventh Army had spoken to Rommel on the telephone. The situation was not as bad as they had thought. Indeed, one could now see that the previous day had been 'a great defensive success'. That battlegroup from the 2nd SS Das Reich Division would not be needed, neither was it now necessary to hurry the 1st SS Adolf Hitler Division across the Orne.

At about midday Dollmann was telling General of the Waffen SS Paul Hausser that he didn't think the II SS Panzer Corps would be called upon. They should be concentrated in such a way that they could be launched into the original panzer counter-offensive, the drive to the sea that would split the Allied armies.

By the afternoon, however, there had been another change. That order countermanding the movement of reinforcements from 1st SS and 2nd SS had to be reinstated. I SS Panzer Corps wanted them for a counter-attack to cut through the Scottish Corridor. By evening the return to reality was complete. The chief staff officer of Seventh Army spoke to Rommel: 'Contrary to what was thought this morning, it is now our opinion that this continued British pressure requires more drastic counter-measures.'[14]

It was a night of movement. Battlegroup Weidinger (2nd SS) took over the Brettevillette–Grainville area (Rauray had fallen to troops of the 49th West Riding Division during the day), and the Panthers and Mark IVs of the Hitler Youth, together with elements of the 26th Grenadiers, went into defence at Hill 112. A Panther company had already moved during the day to Verson and Fontaine Etoupefour, and there were Tigers of the 101 SS Heavy Battalion in this area too. The Hitler Youth divisional headquarters had moved out of what was now the front line at Verson, and was two miles east at Louvigny. Also in defence of Hill 112 were the 83rd Mortar Battalion (7th Mortar Brigade) with fifty-four multiple mortars, the Hitler Youth field artillery withdrawn from south of Cheux, and the 88 mm guns of the Luftwaffe Flak Regiment – one battery lay blown up and abandoned on Hill 112. The hill must be held at all costs! That was the order received by the Hitler Youth Division from the I SS Panzer Corps.

> It is the intention of Montgomery to cross the river Orne and drive forward to the Caen–Falaise highway. The city of Caen, the scene of such hard-fought battles, will then fall into his lap like a ripe piece of fruit.[10]

The news that the British were across the Odon and had their tanks at the foot of Hill 112 was followed late that night by more bad news. Cherbourg had at last fallen to the Americans. A major port for the landing of supplies was in the hands of the Allies.

*

The German hopes that night lay in a pincer attack to be made the next morning by the reinforcements from the 1st SS Adolf Hitler and 2nd SS Das Reich Panzer Divisions. The Scottish Corridor would be cut: the bridgehead would be isolated and destroyed. Two battalions of the 1st SS Panzergrenadier Regiment, supported by tanks from 21st Panzer Division and Hitler Youth Division, would attack west from Verson. They were to push through Mouen and Colleville and meet with Battle-group Weidinger, which would be battling towards them from Grainville in the east. The 83rd Multiple Mortar Battalion and the field guns of the Hitler Youth artillery regiment would give supporting fire.

*

It was past midnight when the 3rd Monmouths were ordered to move forward to the bridgehead. It was trying to rain again. There was empty

(*Above*) Moaning Minnie – a six-barreled multiple mortar loaded and ready to fire.

(*Right*) Loading an 88mm flak gun. In its dual role as an anti-tank gun it was much feared by British tank crews. The gun was mounted high off the ground and gave no protection to the gun crew.

silence in the east. In the west white flares hung in the sky. In the distance, machine-guns chattered nervously.

> We had eaten nothing since dawn, we had just finished digging in for the third time that day, we were tired and hungry. The Herefords and Shropshires were across the Odon. The Scotsmen were holding the western entrance to Tourville, two miles further south. Off we went into the black uncertain night. We stumbled forward over the battle-scarred ground. There were frequent stops. It was difficult to keep the men awake. The moon shone through briefly to reveal a burnt-out Sherman and the waxen face of a dead crewman lying on his back nearby. We came to a dirt track. A whispered message from the rear told us that Sergeant Wheeler and his platoon had dropped off the end of the column. We came to a railway crossing.
>
> There was a very long wait. 'All round defence' came the whispered order. 'Enemy territory – no noise – no digging in.' The hushed night was startled by the words: *'Les Anglais! – Tommy! – Tommy!'* A flood of French welcome followed. Couldn't somebody shut the bastard up? But there was no denying this French farmer the sudden joy of liberation. *'Où sont les Boches?'* he trumpeted. Well, that's what we wanted to know, too, wasn't it!

The Monmouths were too far east. They had wandered off the track in the darkness. They were in the village of Mouen.

Mouen? That was the first objective of the German attack to be launched westwards at dawn across the British line of advance.

I SS Pz CORPS

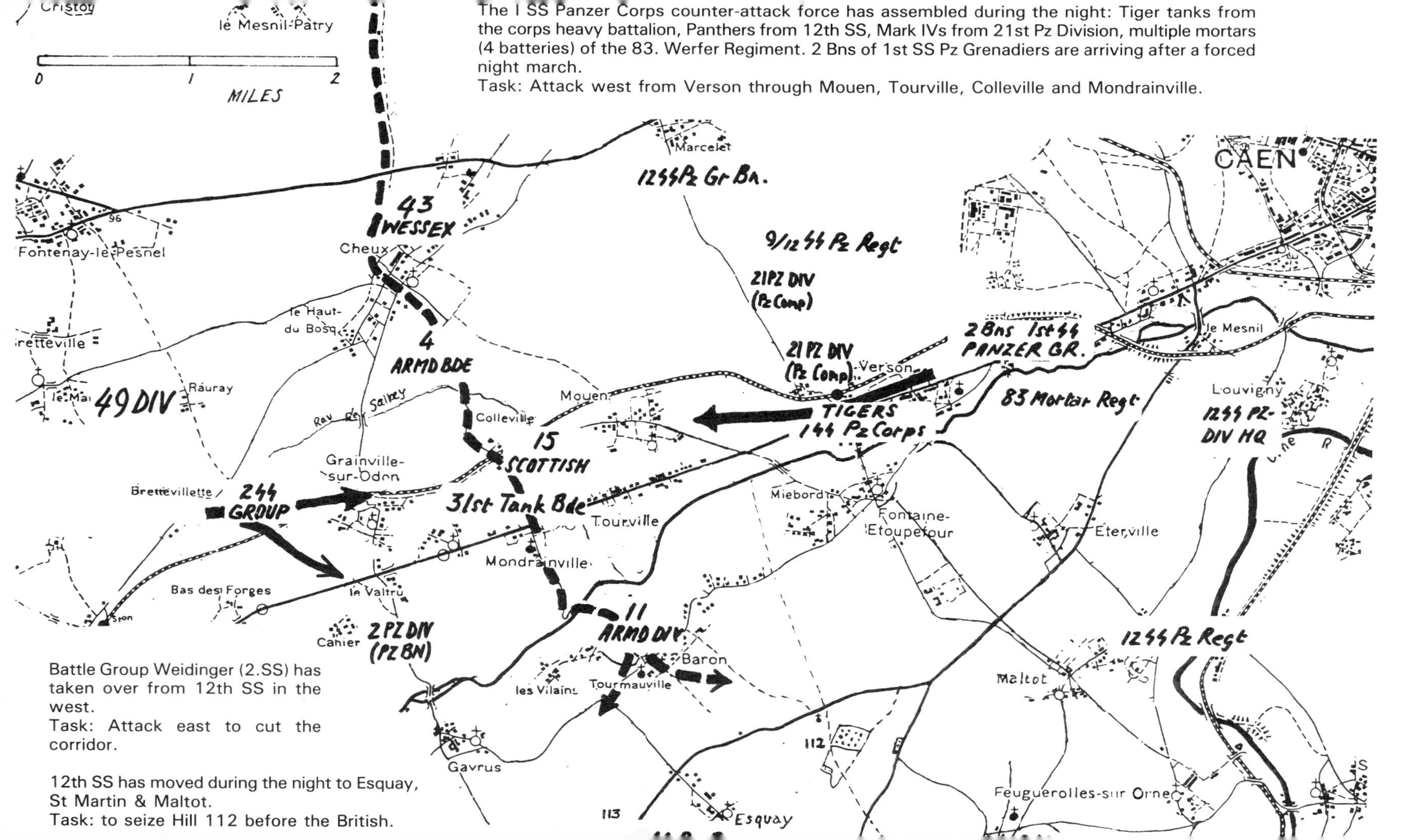
The I SS Panzer Corps counter-attack force has assembled during the night: Tiger tanks from the corps heavy battalion, Panthers from 12th SS, Mark IVs from 21st Pz Division, multiple mortars (4 batteries) of the 83. Werfer Regiment. 2 Bns of 1st SS Pz Grenadiers are arriving after a forced night march.
Task: Attack west from Verson through Mouen, Tourville, Colleville and Mondrainville.
Battle Group Weidinger (2.SS) has taken over from 12th SS in the west.
Task: Attack east to cut the corridor.
12th SS has moved during the night to Esquay, St Martin & Maltot.
Task: to seize Hill 112 before the British.
0
1
2
MILES
le Mesnil-Patry
Fontenay-le-Pesnel
96
43
WESSEX
Cheux
le Haut-du Bosq
4
ARMD BDE
49 DIV
Rauray
le Mai
Marcelet
12SS Pz Gr Bn.
9/12 SS Pz Regt
21PZ DIV
(Pz Comp)
21 PZ DIV
(Pz Comp)
Verson
2 Bns 1st SS
PANZER GR.
le Mesnil
CAEN
TIGERS
1SS Pz Corps
83 Mortar Regt
Louvigny
12SS PZ-DIV HQ
Mouen
Colleville
15
SCOTTISH
Grainville-sur-Odon
Brettevillette
244
GROUP
31st Tank Bde
Tourville
Mondrainville
Miebord
Fontaine-Etoupefour
Eterville
Bas des Forges
le Valtru
Cahier
2 PZ DIV
(PZ BN)
11
ARMD DIV
Baron
Tourmauville
les Vilains
Gavrus
12SS Pz Regt
Maltot
112
113
Esquay
Feuguerolles-sur Orne

CHAPTER SEVEN

Hill 112

28th June 1944

> Field-Marshal von Rundstedt, Commander in Chief West, and Field-Marshal Rommel, Commander of Army Group 'B', are to report to the Fuehrer at Berchtesgaden without delay.

This was the order that confronted the two German military leaders when they awoke on the 28th. It was too dangerous to travel by air. Even an immediate start would not get them to Berchtesgaden by road before nightfall.

Rommel handed over command in Normandy to Dollmann. The latter's brief optimism of the previous day had turned to foreboding. He was a very worried man. Dietrich of the I SS Panzer Corps was pressing for help:

> Even the arrival of the 1st SS Adolf Hitler Panzer Division will not halt the British at Baron; they will push through to the river Orne, and Caen will be lost; only the II SS Panzer Corps can prevent this happening.[17]

Before he left Normandy, Rommel gave permission to throw in the II SS Panzer Corps. Its commander, Obergruppenfuehrer Paul Hausser, reported that he would not be ready to attack before seven the next morning.

Three hours after Rommel had left with von Rundstedt for Germany, Dollmann was dead. The entry in the war diary of the Seventh Army states that he died of a heart attack; we now know that the strain had been too much; he had committed suicide.

> It is the order of the Fuehrer that SS Obergruppenfuehrer and General of the Waffen SS Hausser take over command. The Fuehrer

> further orders that he assume temporary command of the whole Normandy front until the return of Field-Marshal Rommel.[17]

At a time when the German Army in Normandy was facing its worst crisis since the invasion, not one of the top three military leaders was there. Hausser, just arrived from the Russian front, had been promoted out of the command of the key formation in the coming counter-attack. The awesome responsibility for the whole battle was now his.

Papa Hausser, as he was called by his Waffen SS soldiers, had become the first general of the Waffen SS to be given command of a German army. He was a brave and experienced soldier with a military career that went back to before the first world war. A lieutenant-general in the Reichswehr, Germany's pre-war army, he had left to become, at Hitler's call, the founder and military trainer of what was now the Waffen SS. The command of the II SS Panzer Corps was taken over by the commander of 9th SS, Wilhelm Bittrich.

*

Captain Mike Peppiatt, the artillery forward observation officer with the Gordons who had been taken prisoner south of Cheux, was being held captive in a house in the village of Baron. All day on the 27th the village had been under intermittent British artillery fire :

> Shells again. Another Yoke target. Wearily back to the slit trench for another spell of misery. . . Back to the house again to rest . . . more shells . . . the trench. . . On and on all day . . . exhausted mentally and physically.

On the morning of the 28th he awoke to a surprise :

> Where am I? Yes – the house – prisoners – four of us. The sun is shining – Must have slept all night – let's have a look outside – Look – there ! Soldiers – yes – they're in khaki – Yes they're British alright !

The Shropshire Light Infantry, who had arrived during the night, viewed Captain Peppiatt and his driver with suspicion :

> 'Us? Spies? Nonsense, man ! Take me to your commanding officer !'

*

The Shropshires and Herefords had had no sleep that night. What with digging in and chasing after German stragglers they were fully occupied. And there were the Moaning Minnies, too. They listened aghast at the screams hurtling across the night sky towards them; the multi-toned crescendo seemed always to be accelerating towards just their piece of ground. They pressed themselves flat against the earth as the explosions broke in an erratic cluster around them.

It was just after dawn that fifteen German soldiers turned up at the farm of Madame Villedieu and asked for milk. She had quite a shock. '*Tommies ici!*' she exclaimed. '*Uns egal!*' (All the same to us!) answered one.

Even as he spoke the shooting started. Madame ran for the shelter of her kitchen. There was not much comfort there. Machine-gun fire rattled past the window, and tiles were displaced on the roof by exploding grenades. She ran to her neighbour. But the battle spread there, too. When all was at last quiet again they went outside. Cows in the field had been killed. In the courtyard lay two dead British soldiers.

Captain Mearns, the medical officer, had to make a dive for safety when bursts of automatic fire tore through the medical aid post. Two stretcher bearers were hit and wounded. 'From underneath the medical truck I could see three or four German soldiers in camouflaged uniforms amongst the trees.'

Men of the Rifle Brigade searched through the densely wooded area of the Odon valley. Every man of the leading section was wounded. Others were sent to help:

> In a fresh outbreak of machine-gun and mortar fire, Michael Lane was wounded together with several others. Micky McCrae went down in the scout car. A bullet entered his knee. He was brought back looking very white.[18*]

The Shermans of the Hussars, expecting a counter-attack, had moved before dawn to defensive positions on the perimeter of the bridgehead. No counter-attack came, but the light of day revealed two German panzers, twelve hundred yards away on the high ground near Esquay. They must have arrived during the night and halted, unaware of their exposed position. The 23rd Hussars opened fire on them and claimed to have hit both.

They had indeed arrived during the night. The Mark IV Hitler Youth Panzer Battalion had withdrawn under cover of darkness, and

* Major Noel Bell, 8th Rifle Brigade.

with some twenty panzers still fit for action was moving to defend Hill 112 and prevent it falling into British hands. The ten Mark IVs of the 5th Company had halted at Esquay to await further orders. The panzer crews, exhausted after three days of continuous battle, had for the most part collapsed into a deep sleep. At nine o'clock they were on the move again. They formed up about a mile south of the 'little box-shaped wood' on Hill 112. Further east, at St Martin, was a company of the Hitler Youth Panthers. At ten o'clock the order to advance was given: objective – the summit of 112.

A squadron of the Hussars and a company of the Rifle Brigade in halftracks and carriers had already moved up the slope from the other side. Forward to the river Orne! This was General O'Connor's order. The crossing of the Orne was the second phase of the Epsom operation, and he was anxious to get started. The summit of Hill 112 covered a large area. It was flat in some places, concave in others. There were some hedges and embankments. It was otherwise devoid of cover. When the Hussars poked their nose over on to the enemy side there was a violent reaction.

One tank was hit by a fifty-millimetre shot that broke its track. Lieutenant Cochrane's tank was hit and destroyed. The crew got out and came under heavy fire from both sides. To get some protection they dug shallow trenches for themselves with jacknives and fingernails.

Lieutenant Bishop sat watching in his tank as men of the Rifle Brigade winkled out a German observation post:

> Suddenly a scraggy-looking beggar in field grey appeared from a hedge, hatless and with his hands in the air. He was rushed off at the point of a bayonet. He kept looking back, frightened, or perhaps worried about what was happening to his companion. A moment later, two more, one an officer, were captured.

This was an observation post of the German mortar batteries in the Eterville area. At nine o'clock the field telephone of No 6 Battery rang. It was answered by Feldwebel Doorn. What he heard sent him running to find his commander, Hauptmann Gengl:

> Sir, the British are on top of the hill. A Sherman tank has stopped just five yards from one of our observation posts. He says for God's sake not to ring – they'll hear it. He'll try to get back somehow. He doesn't know what's happened to Lieutenant Wernicke and Lieutenant Nitschmann. He thinks they must have been overrun.[19]

Men of the Rifle Brigade on Hill 112 have a look at the letters just arrived from the UK. In the background is a halftrack.

Men of the Rifle Brigade prepare a meal for their mates in action on Hill 112. The fourteen-man pack in the foreground contained sufficient food for that number for one day. The tinned food was of excellent quality; included in the box were cigarettes, boiled sweets and toilet paper.

Feldwebel Doorn was sent up the hill with a patrol. It failed to get to the top. British machine-guns opened up. Bullets ripped through the corn stalks where the patrol lay hidden. Corporal Trautz and another man were wounded. It was only with great difficulty that Doorn got back with the wounded men. He reported to Hauptmann Gengl:

> It's not just a couple of tanks up there! Tommy's got anti-tank guns and part of a machine-gun unit.[19]

The German Mark IV panzers climbed the hill from the south unseen. They were hidden by the trees of the little wood, which hung down on their side of the slope. They fired with machine-guns and cannon into the trees and bushes to clear it of any British who might be there. Oberscharfuehrer (Sergeant) Willy Kretschmar was one of the panzer commanders:

> When I came to the end of the cover provided by the little wood, I halted and had a good look round. With my binoculars I searched the country stretching away to our left, looking for tanks and anti-tank guns. Nothing suspicious! 'Panzer advance!' I shouted. We had advanced ten or fifteen metres when there was a sudden crash. The sparks flew. We had been hit from the right. 'Reverse!' I shouted. Sturmmann (Private) Schneider reacted like lightning. Back we shot at full speed. Back into the cover of the wood. And only just in time! The 'Engländer' almost got us! A hair's breadth in front of our panzer, armour-piercing solid shot was tearing horrible black furrows in the green grass.[9]

Six new Shermans had arrived on the other side of the hill. They replaced losses in the two previous days of battle. They were crewed by men of the Hussars who had been left out of battle, and were some of the longest-standing members of the regiment. Three were knocked out within twenty minutes of arrival. Corporal Clear's tank was the first to go. He had pushed his nose just a little too far over the crest. Then Captain R. Clark's tank was hit. Lieutenant Bishop was just to his rear:

> I saw Bob's tank was beginning to catch fire. His troop sergeant jumped out of his own tank and ran over to help him. They were then hidden from me behind a hedge.

Although the sergeant and one of the drivers managed to get Captain Clark out of the turret, he was in a bad way and died later.

The third to go was the tank of Lieutenant Helyar. He, too, died of his wounds.

Enemy mortar bombs and shells were pounding the hilltop. A lot of solid armour-piercing shot was being thrown at the British tanks. The little wood hanging back on the enemy side was the object of the greatest suspicion. Major Blacker of the Hussars, convinced that it was a Tiger tank he had seen there, left his Sherman behind and went forward on foot with men of the Rifle Brigade. They got into the wood and spotted a German tank lurking in the undergrowth at the far end. They couldn't bring any weapon to bear, and as no tank could survive the move across the open summit, the RAF was brought in. The rocket-firing Typhoons swooped down with a terrifying roar and left the wood hidden in a great pall of dust and smoke.

> We turned into a square field surrounded by trees and bushes. There was only one gap, and a steepish bank had to be crossed to gain entrance. We were on top of Hill 112.[18]*

There was a lull, a tense, uncomfortable calm. Anti-tank guns were dragged into position. The riflemen dug in. The bombardment started again. Spasmodic at first, then increasing to a great intensity. There were casualties. Vehicles were hit and burning. The tanks were firing back, more in anger and frustration than with any hope of hitting a target.

But the Hussars had been more successful than they knew. The German attempt to regain the top of Hill 112 had failed. Of the ten Mark IVs that had that morning arrived at Esquay, only four were still in action. The others were either battle casualties or had dropped out with mechanical defects. Tank units in battle, both British and German, were in permanent flux. Some technical faults were quickly cured, and the tanks were back in action within the hour; tanks knocked out one day could be back in action the next.

The Panzer IVs of the Hitler Youth No 5 Company withdrew eastwards for three quarters of a mile to a fold in the ground which hid them from Hill 112. A mortar battery had been firing from there; it was packing up to move to a new position. The Panzer IVs drew up alongside a hedge. 'I lay down utterly exhausted and went to sleep.' That remark by one member of tank crew, summed up the feelings of

* Major Noel Bell, 8th Rifle Brigade.

them all. Nothing is as important as sleep to those who have been deprived of it. Battles are invariably contests between similar sleep-starved, weary and overwrought groups of soldiers. When the sleep drive takes over, fear of the enemy, of the Moaning Minnies, of the shellfire and the anti-tank guns takes a poor second place.

By midday the sleeping tank crews had been shaken back to reality, a world of crackling earphones, of crashing and banging, of sweat and tension. Another attempt was made to take the little wood:

> My gunner, Willi Schnittfinke, reported a defect in the electric firing mechanism. We had to halt, and after a quick repair we were some distance behind the three panzers manoeuvring in front of us. Hauptscharfuehrer Mueller was also hanging back behind Porsch and Kunze. Kunze, in the leading panzer, referring no doubt to those hanging back, shouted over the wireless: *'Scheiss egal! Panzer marsch!'* [It's all the bloody same to me! Advance!] Two hundred yards from the little wood Kunze's panzer was knocked out. Only the gunner and driver baled out. Groeter, the driver, was visibly shaken. He said the shell had gone clean between his legs.*

That this attack like the first came to nothing is not surprising. By this time the British were in overwhelming strength. The Hussars were complete with all three squadrons on the hill, and had brought up in addition some self-propelled anti-tank guns. But, exposed at the end of a narrow salient, they were under observation and fire from all directions except the north. There were German tanks and anti-tank guns in the wooded country to the north-east, and British reconnaissance tanks that entered Gavrus in the west, were soon chased out by German armour.

*

Dawn had found the 3rd Monmouths in the village of Mouen, on the eastern side of the corridor. This was 'no man's land'; it lay between the German front just west of Verson, and the edge of the Scottish Corridor at Colleville. One company was ordered to hold it until relieved later in the day by a battalion from the 15th Scottish. The bulk of the battalion marched out with the dawn to take up positions just north of the Tourmauville bridge. Fifty men had been lost in the night. With them was Sergeant Frank Wheeler:

* Untersturmfuehrer (Lieutenant) Kaendler, 12th SS Panzer Regt.

Some idiot had fallen asleep during one of the long halts, and the rest of the battalion had gone on without us. I didn't know where we were, where we were going, or where the enemy was. I put the men in all round defence and waited for the light of day. The men had had nothing to eat all day, they had dug in three times, and they were browned off. They kept pestering me to let them smoke. In the end I gave in. 'Three at a time,' I said, 'with gas capes over your heads!' At dawn we found 'C' Company near a railway line. There wasn't a sound and no sign of the enemy. I wanted to stay with 'C' Company, but Major Richards insisted that I chase after the battalion and catch them up. Suddenly the two scouts I had put out in front signalled danger. A strong force of infantry was coming along the track in our direction. We took cover and prepared to have a go. But when they appeared they had British tin hats. Our own battalion! And a bloody good thing, too!

*

The German Seventh Army had wanted the counter-attack to go in at night. That was the wish of Obersturmbannfuehrer (Lieutenant-Colonel) Albert Frey, who had arrived at the 12th SS Hitler Youth headquarters on the evening of the 27th to plan it. A stop must be put to the advance of the British VIII Corps. The pressure was on. This was the only action that could force the British to look over their shoulder and pause. This would give the German command time to bring in the II SS Panzer Corps, which had now been released for action against the British salient.

Two battalions of panzer grenadiers from the 1st SS Adolf Hitler Panzer Division had been rushed on ahead across the Orne to make the counter-attack. Delayed by attacks from low-flying bombers of the RAF, they had failed to arrive in time to fight under cover of darkness. The 21st Panzer Division had sent two Mark IV panzer companies, both much under strength. The Hitler Youth had contributed a Panther company and there were some Tigers from the 101 SS Heavy Battalion (troops of the I SS Panzer Corps). Artillery support was to come from a regiment of the Hitler Youth Division and multiple mortars from the 7th Werfer Brigade. Obersturmfuehrer Albert Frey had wanted to wait until the arrival of the 1st SS Panzer Division artillery, but there could be no delay; the I SS Panzer Corps, the German Seventh Army and Army Group 'B' were all breathing down Frey's neck; the counter-attack must be launched as soon as possible.

The panzers and panzer grenadiers were to advance from Verson, cutting westwards along the main road and the railway line. The first objective was Mouen. The attackers would then take Tourville and Colleville and meet up with Battlegroup Weidinger (2nd SS), who would have advanced east from Grainville to reach Mondrainville. The British spearhead south of the Odon would then be cut off. The advance of VIII Corps would be halted. The British would have to turn and deal with the threat in their rear. Into the resulting disorganisation and confusion would then be launched the forty thousand men of the II SS Panzer Corps, 9th SS and 10th SS Panzer Divisions.

Wireless operator in one of the Mark IVs of 21st Panzer Division was nineteen-year-old Werner Kortenhaus:

> We advanced at nine o'clock in the morning, moving along the railway line with the grenadiers. The Panther tanks were further left. My company only had five panzers still fit for action. Almost immediately we ran into fierce opposition. The grenadiers came and asked us to help them. They said they had surrounded a group of British infantry in Mouen.

The many lanes of Mouen were alive with the German panzers and grenadiers. They had taken over Mademoiselle Robert's house for their wounded. She had to fetch water for them from the well in the courtyard. A young German soldier was standing there, shouting defiance and curses at each shell that fell. A panzer had bogged down in the village pond, near the baker's shop. When a British tank suddenly appeared it was hit and burst into a ball of flame and black smoke. Two men baled out, one with his clothes on fire. The other was shot as he sought the cover of the wood nearby.

Private Evans was with the company of Monmouths left in Mouen:

> We were not properly dug-in. Many were killed or wounded in the heavy bombardment. A light recce tank arrived – one of ours. 'Get back, they've got heavy tanks!' we shouted. But it stayed and was soon hit and in flames.

Twenty-three Monmouths were killed. Only Major Richards* and fourteen men got out. Gwilliam Evans was taken prisoner:

* Major Richards was killed by shell fire two days later.

> We looked after our wounded as best we could. We carried one on a door used as a stretcher. Later the SS general saw some of his soldiers take our cigarettes. He was very angry. He pointed to our shoulder flashes, said something, and made them give the cigarettes back. His name was Kurt something or the other. He was a gentleman.

On the western side of the corridor there was complete confusion. Battlegroup Weidinger arrived to find that Grainville was already in the hands of the Cameronians, and half a mile south, on the main Caen road, they bumped into the Seaforth Highlanders, who were advancing to take the village of le Valtru. These Scottish troops, unaware that they were opposed by a German counter-attack intent on getting to Mondrainville, could only wonder at the sudden increase in enemy activity. The whole area north of the main road from Grainville to Mouen had erupted in battle. It was close country of farms, orchards and narrow lanes that twisted and turned in confusion. Panthers and panzer grenadiers had managed to infiltrate as far as Mondrainville, which still held German stragglers from the fighting the day before. The Glasgow Highlanders, holding the eastern edge of the vital track leading south from Cheux, were reporting heavy battle in the Mouen area just in front of them. Later in the morning, with the Monmouths overrun, they, too, came under increasing pressure from the German counter-attack coming in from the east.

Eight miles to the rear, in the ruins of the little village of Putot-en-Bessin, General O'Connor was in conference at the headquarters of the 15th Scottish Division. He was giving the 'bigger picture'.

The 49th West Riding Division had failed to keep pace with the advance, and there were now four miles of unprotected flank south of Rauray. The western edge of the Scottish corridor was boiling over, and there had been heavy and confused fighting in the area of Grainville and le Valtru since dawn. There were many Germans still in this area, and they seemed to be growing in numbers and to have plenty of tank support. On the eastern side British reconnaissance tanks were reporting strong enemy infantry and panzer groups in the area Mouen. The British spearhead across the Odon was still relying for all its supplies on the one muddy, narrow track through Cheux, where soft vehicles and tanks were 'milling round like the traffic in Piccadilly Circus'. This corridor south was less than a mile wide in places, and was vulnerable to enemy attack.

There were other, more ominous signs. The RAF was reporting a great bottleneck of German armoured columns moving through Villers-Bocage towards the battle area. There had been a great increase in the activity of the German flak, and German fighter planes were appearing in greater numbers.

These were the factors that now caused O'Connor to bring the advance south across the Orne to a halt. It would be temporary. Present positions were to be held. When enemy resistance north of the river Odon had been cleared up, and the threat to the western side of the corridor had disappeared, the advance would be pushed on across the Orne as originally planned.

Early in the afternoon the Hussars on Hill 112 were reporting a shortage of ammunition. It was impossible to send lorries up to them with a new supply. At three o'clock they withdrew after handing over to the 3rd Royal Tanks.

The 23rd Hussars found themselves back in reserve in a field near Tourmauville. It was their first respite after three days and three nights in battle. Seventy-two members of tank crew had been lost; thirty-three had been killed, six were missing.

> As the tanks drew up along the perimeter of a small field, begrimed faces wore an expression of intense relief; 'So I did make it!' The colonel walked round chatting to the men, asking them how they had got on. It was a bedraggled group of men that surrounded him, clothed in the comfortable untidiness necessary for fighting a tank. The dust of Normandy, which was to irritate us through these early battles, had got into their clothes, and into the chapped pores of their skins, had reddened their eyes and parched throats – many commanders had practically lost their voices.[1]

During the afternoon the 3rd Royal Tanks reported sightings of Panther tanks west of Esquay, and Tigers and other armour in the area of Maltot.

At half past four the Mark IVs of the Hitler Youth, increased in strength to fifteen, again attempted to climb the southern slope of 112. They came once again under heavy fire from armour-piercing shot, had casualties, and withdrew. In the evening the Hitler Youth Panzer Regiment commander visited them, praised their efforts, and told them that thirty-six British tanks had been counted on the crest and northern slopes.

Still sweating it out with the tanks on the top of the hill were the infantrymen of the 8th Rifle Brigade. Huddled in their shallow trenches they had been sorely troubled by the Moaning Minnies :

> It was a diabolical sound, like that of a giant retching, repeated several times in quick succession. There followed a great whistling, culminating in a devilish scream.[18*]

As it grew dark the British withdrew. The sign of movement brought a renewed outburst of enemy hate, and the Rifle Brigade made the descent amidst the screams and whistles of exploding mortar bombs. Two ditched anti-tank guns and an immobilised halftrack had to be left behind.

> There was much confusion. Nobody seemed to be sure what was happening or what the form was. Brian approached, supported under the arms by two of his section leaders. The parts of his face not covered with mud or blood showed through deathly pale. We gave him a shot of brandy from a flask; he coughed. The trucks and carriers turned and made their way back through the orchard. We saw a halftrack burning, one of 'H' Company's. Ammunition was exploding, and the blazing tyres made vivid circles of flames. We made laager, and attempted to find order out of chaos. A feeling of depression swept through us. There were only two officers left. The morning, just a few hours behind us, seemed another age.[18†]

As that darkness was falling, so Untersturmfuehrer (Lieutenant) Willi Kaendler of the Hitler Youth Panzer Regiment drove up the southern slope of 112 in a Volkswagen in search of his friend Helmut Kunze, who had failed to bale out when his Mark IV had that morning been knocked out. A recce group had reported a knocked out Panzer IV with its engine still running and a dead man in the turret. Kaendler found it :

> It was, indeed, that of Kunze. In front of the panzer lay the loader, Howe, dead, on his back, with blue eyes open. There were flecks of blood on his face. On the commander's seat was huddled Helmet Kunze, dead. The shell seemed to have struck him right in the back. On his right was the dead gunner. The motor was still running.[9]

Kaendler drove the tank with its dead crewmen back down the hill.

* Major Noel Bell, 8th Rifle Brigade.
† Major Noel Bell, 8th Rifle Brigade.

Near the bottom it ran out of petrol and had to be towed the rest of the way. The dead crewmen were buried in the garden of Château Coultru.

*

Nightfall signalled the failure of the German counter-attack to cut through the Scottish Corridor from Mouen in the east and from Grainville in the west. The company of Monmouths left in Mouen had absorbed the first shock of the German onslaught and had been wiped out in the process. It was late afternoon when the 10th Highland Light Infantry learned about it the hard way. They had been ordered to relieve the Monmouths, and were marching through the standing corn, moving down towards the railway line, when they suddenly faced a wall of machine-gun fire at almost point-blank range. Some were killed or wounded; others went to ground as death scythed through the corn stalks above them. Sergeant Green could see just ahead of him the bodies of men of 'A' Company; the 'white hair of Lance-Corporal McCloy – now vividly blotched with blood' stood out clearly. A rushing blast of air indicated that a solid anti-tank shot had passed just overhead.

Werner Kortenhaus and the five panzers of 21st Panzer Division were still halted in the triangular field beyond the railway line:

> We received a direct hit. The battle had suddenly flared up again. We couldn't traverse the gun. The turret was jammed. As we pulled back we were hit again, this time in the rear. Fortunately the shot bounced off. An hour later, with the turret freed we were back in

'The crew got out and shortened the track with the battle raging all round.' This Panzer IV of 21st Panzer Division, commanded by Unteroffizier Wenz, was detracked but able to withdraw after repairs on the battlefield.

> the thick of the battle. One of our panzers was in flames. Another slowly backed out of the battle with the commander, Eichler, lying dead in the turret. He had been decapitated by a shell as he was looking out over the top. A third was hit. The crew got out and shortened the track with the battle raging all round. They got their panzer going, but it had to pull out of the fray.

All five panzers were knocked out or damaged, and Kortenhaus himself was out of the battle when he caught his foot in the panzer track.

> We had fired very little. The British kept firing smoke shells and we couldn't see, except for an occasional misty outline.

Nightfall found the two sides still locked in battle on the railway line. The Highland Light Infantry were ordered to pull back to Colleville. The last of their many casualties was the 'father of the regiment', Captain Bain, the battalion quartermaster. In the dark he ran into the enemy and was killed.

The Germans remained in possession of Mouen: the battle report reads:

> Our counter-attack on the Caen road was brought to a halt by enemy tank attacks on the line Mouen–Odon valley. Bitter fighting went on until after nightfall.[15]

Major General Ivor Thomas of the 43rd Wessex Division had been ordered to put in a fresh attack during the night with a brigade of infantry. What had twelve hours earlier fallen into British hands without a shot being fired, had then been lost for want of prompt action. It would now take a brigade to win it back again.

While the British were planning a night attack on Mouen from the north, so the forty thousand men of the II SS Panzer Corps were moving through the darkness on the western side of the Scottish Corridor in preparation for the counter-attack they were to make the next day. 10th SS Frundsberg Division would operate south of the Odon; its objectives would be Gavrus and Baron. 9th SS Hohenstaufen Division would be north of the river and cut through Cheux and Mouen to Carpiquet, where contact would be made with the 12th SS Hitler Youth Division. The 2nd SS battlegroup (Weidinger) would give flank protection on the left. The 7th Mortar Brigade was expected during the night, and the 8th was already in position.

Nothing less than the destruction of the British VIII Corps was the aim.

CHAPTER EIGHT

Monty's nose takes a knocking

29th June 1944

'If only we were out of this ghastly hole,' thought General Kurt Meyer of the 12th SS Hitler Youth Division. 'The old walls close in like a trap.'[10*]

There was an unbroken din of artillery fire. It was seven o'clock in the morning in Verson. A German halftrack was ablaze in the middle of one of the narrow streets. Ammunition was exploding and flying in all directions. Further along the road an ambulance was on fire. Both were the victims of an Allied fighter bomber that had dropped out of the clear blue sky like a hawk.

*

A mile to the west the 43rd Wessex Division was attacking at Mouen, and was putting down one of those massive artillery 'stonks' that came as such a shock to German soldiers when they first experienced it. 'Had it not been for their artillery we would have taught the Tommies to swim!' wrote one Rottenfuehrer (SS Corporal) in a letter home. The grass is always greener on the other side of the hill. 'Had it not been for their mortars,' Tommy might have replied, 'we would have chased them out of Normandy a lot earlier!'†

Air domination was another matter. There the German soldier had every reason to feel let down: 'Our so-called Luftwaffe never puts in an appearance!' – 'There was nothing like this in Russia!' And there is this comment from a British soldier who, as a prisoner, experienced the sharp end of those fighter-bomber raids behind the German front: 'One wonders what we would have been like faced with that kind of air domination.'

* Panzermeyer.
† German mortars accounted for 70% of British casualties in Normandy.

It was the 1st Worcesters who got into Mouen. They had come down over the crest in the north while the German defence was taking cover from the massive 'stonk' of the divisional artillery plus two medium regiments and the massed mortars of three infantry battalions. Smoke mixed with the high explosive was increasing the confusion. The German defensive barrage fell in the wrong place; in the west, where the Highland Light Infantry had made their attack the evening before. By eleven o'clock in the morning it was all over. Mouen was in the hands of the Worcesters for a loss of only four men killed. The smoke had drifted away to reveal a scene of great carnage.

Dozens of bodies were lying in the area of the railway line. One ditch, a mass of bomb and shell craters, was lined with the dead of the Monmouths, killed there the morning before. A panzer had pushed its way half through the nearby hedge; its turret was turned to one side, and its long gun hung there, still threatening. Nearby were another nine bodies of Monmouths and another destroyed panzer. There was a narrow lane and some farm buildings. The dead of the Highland Light Infantry were 'hanging out of windows and from doorways and lying in the roadway itself'. There were seven or eight destroyed panzers in the village, 'including three enormous Tigers'.

Following up behind the Worcesters were the Somersets and Wiltshires. Together they pushed south across the main Caen road and down into the valley of the Odon. By late in the afternoon they had crossed over and widened the 11th Armoured bridgehead eastwards to the village of Fontaine-Etoupefour. Verson, however, remained in German hands.

It was the Royal Artillery that put the Worcesters into Mouen with such few casualties. 'The closer you are, the safer you are!' That had been the slogan on those exercises in the UK in which battalions were taught to move close behind a moving barrage of live ammunition. 'Where will Jerry be? Keeping his bloody head down!' It was proving itself in practice, but it needed a well-disciplined battalion to follow up closely, and it didn't always work smoothly. Infantrymen were killed and wounded when inaccurate gunlaying or worn gun barrels caused shells to fall short. The German defence tactic of allowing their infantry to shelter in deep shell-proof bunkers until the barrage passed on proved not infrequently ineffective. The German defenders rushed out to find the 'Tommies' already there or within easy striking distance.*

* German soldiers came to the mistaken conclusion that the last few shells before the barrage lifted and moved on were harmless 'flash-bangs' that allowed the British to move in close without danger.

*

'A man nearby said softly: "Oh Christ!" It reflected the feelings of us all. But it was not for us to reason why.'[18*]

Two companies of the Rifle Brigade had been ordered to move forward out of the bridgehead and take up positions on Hill 112 again. The halftrack and the two guns ditched and left up there the night before were to be recovered, and there was a plan to occupy the little wood lying back on the enemy side.

The depressing thought of another day on the hilltop seemed at first to have been misplaced. The Rifle Brigade reached the summit without a shot being fired.

The 3rd Royal Tanks were already there, with their Sherman tanks in hull-down positions. The Rifle Brigade moved into the trenches they had dug the day before:

> Shelling and mortaring commenced, varying in pitch from time to time. Bren carriers were blown bodily off the ground, but there were no direct hits. Our mortars, working with those of 'H' Company, put down a steady stream of fire. Sergeant Hollands continued to operate the mortars until wounded by shrapnel. Naish, leaning against a bank above his slit trench, was holding the wireless head-phones in his hand, the better to hear any approaching shells, when there was an explosion nearby; shrapnel tore through the bakelite, leaving in his hand only the metal band.[18†]

That little wood lying back from the crest, the morning before a waving green silhouette against the blue sky, was beginning to look bedraggled and distorted.

*

> Men of the II SS Panzer Corps, you can be proud of your success in battle. Your Fuehrer now calls you to new tasks. I know that you will fulfil them in the spirit of our motto, that no soldier in the world shall be better than the soldiers of Adolf Hitler, our leader.[3]

With the praises of the commander of the German armies of the Ukraine ringing in their ears, the men of the 9th SS Hohenstaufen and 10th SS Frundsberg Panzer Divisions had left Russia to start the long

* Major Noel Bell, 8th Rifle Brigade.
† Major Noel Bell, 8th Rifle Brigade.

journey back to France. Morale was high after a first heady taste of victory against the Russians.

Now, seventeen days later, Hitler was about to launch them into the most powerful German counter-attack of the Normandy campaign. He was confident that the fighting qualities of his Waffen SS élite would be more than a match for the average Allied soldier, and that this blow against the British would lead on to the final defeat of the Normandy invasion.

SS Panzer Divisions were powerful fighting formations. Both the 9th SS Hohenstaufen and the 10th SS Frundsberg had over seventeen thousand men when they arrived in Normandy from Russia.* An SS panzer division had almost twice as many infantrymen as its British counterpart, and although it was outnumbered in the size of its tank force, those it did have were armed with a more powerful gun and many had thicker armour.

The inferiority of the Allied tanks was clearly recognised by both the British and Americans before the invasion. It was information not unnaturally suppressed from newspaper and radio reports. When criticism began to filter back from tank commanders fighting in Normandy, it was characteristically dismissed by Montgomery as 'alarmist' and the work of 'officers with no responsibility and little battle experience'. II SS Panzer Corps had picked up on its journey through France ninety new Panthers from the depot at Mailly-le-Camp, and this must have brought the tank strength of the corps to well over two hundred.

But with the last of the 10th SS Frundsberg troops only just arriving in Normandy, and the Tiger tank battalion still far away, the II SS Panzer Corps was being ordered to counter-attack before it was ready. In vain had been the plea for delay. The German front had fallen apart. Only immediate action could prevent the situation deteriorating still further. Success now could turn the battle around. It could lead to the defeat of the Allies in Normandy. Delay might see the opportunity disappear, perhaps for ever.

All night long the armoured columns of the Frundsberg and Hohenstaufen Divisions had been moving into position along the western side of the Scottish Corridor. The dawn broke and they were still not ready. The 7th Werfer Brigade, which was to support the counter-attack with over a hundred multiple mortars, was only just arriving. The attack could not go in at seven o'clock. There would be a two hour delay.

* On 1/6/44 the 9th SS strength was 17,612; that of 10th SS was 17,023. 11th Armoured had started Epsom with 12,715 men.

When nine o'clock approached it was put back again to one o'clock in the afternoon.

The morning had started quietly enough for the British on the western flank. It held all the promise of a fine hot day.

At ten o'clock General O'Connor called a meeting of his senior commanders. His orders were simple. No further advance. Prepare for an enemy onslaught from the west. Dig in and strengthen the defences. The order to the 4th Armoured Brigade to join 11th Armoured Division in a push forward to the river Orne is cancelled. The 44th Royal Tanks, already there, will stay. The other two tank battalions will move immediately into positions of support for the Scottish infantry holding the western side of the corridor.

Five days earlier Montgomery had learned through Ultra that units of the 9th SS and 10th SS Panzer Divisions were arriving in Normandy on transfer from the Russian front. That news had been passed on to General Dempsey, commander of the British Second Army. There it had stopped, for in order to maintain the secrecy of this important source of information it was restricted to army commanders. We must presume that O'Connor had no knowledge of it. He knew, however, from RAF reports, that German troop columns were converging on his front and that a threat was building up in the west. And we may be sure that both Dempsey and Montgomery, who knew more, must have been encouraging a halt to the advance. The British could not afford to lose this battle.

The key position in the coming struggle would be the village of Cheux. All the food and ammunition for the troops further south and in the bridgehead had to pass through Cheux. But the Germans controlled the road leading into the village from the south-west, and they were less than a mile away. A successful enemy push here would bring the collapse of the British position further south. This vital road was the boundary between the 15th Scottish and the 49th West Riding Division.

At eleven o'clock in the morning the Royal Scots pushed troops forward into Belval farm and the adjoining wood. From there they could fire on to the road and keep visual contact with the Tyneside Scottish on the other side. The Germans immediately attacked them with panzers and infantry. By midday the Royal Scots were under heavy artillery and mortar fire, were having difficulty in holding on and were calling for help from the men of the West Riding Division across the road. They had bumped trouble further south also. There they had crossed the railway line intending to occupy the farm buildings at les

‘All food and ammunition . . . had to pass through Cheux.’

The muddy track from Cheux to Colleville. The skyline is the higher ground of ring contour 100, where the British tanks were held up on the first day of battle. French refugees from Verson are fleeing the battle area.

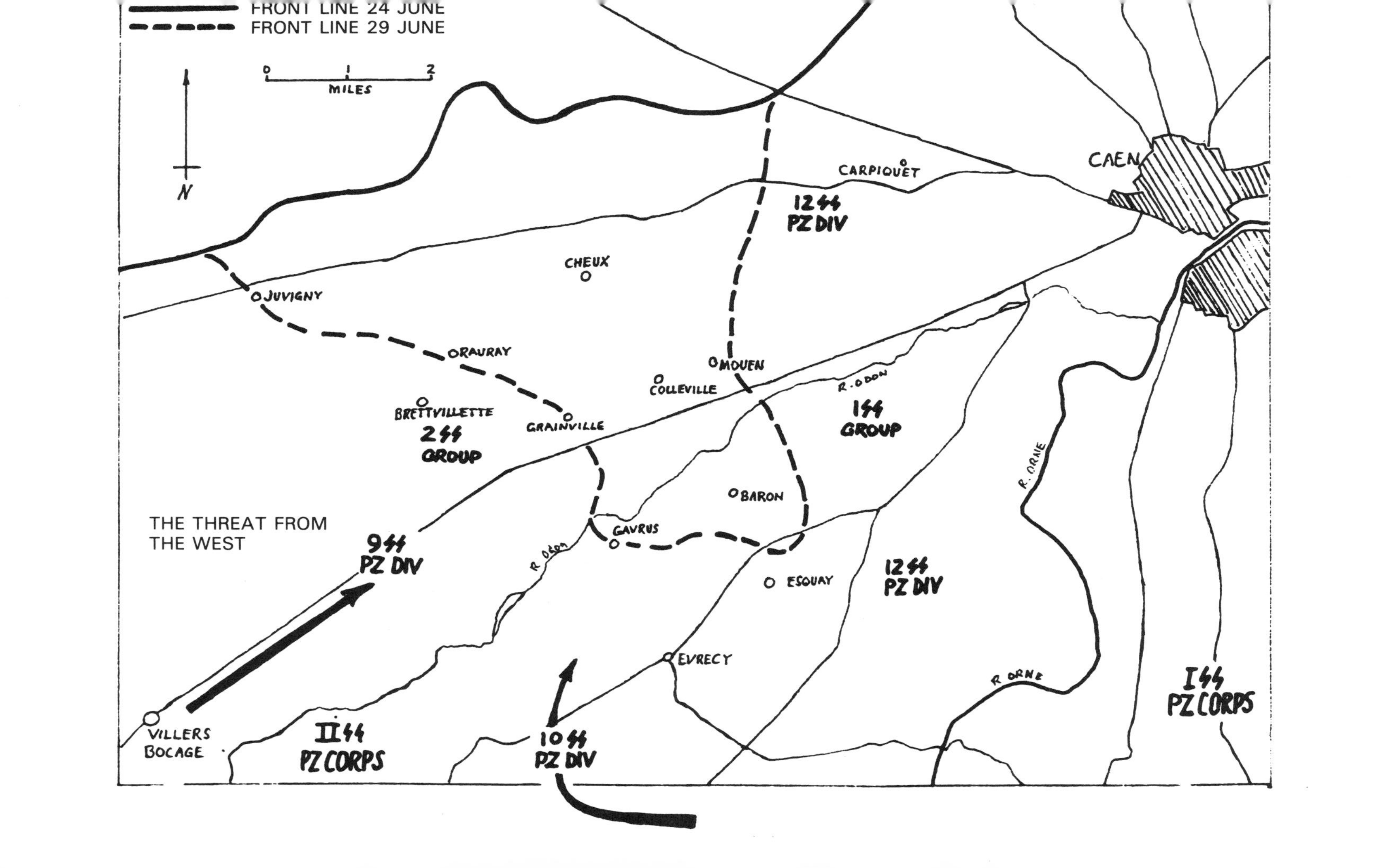

THE THREAT FROM THE WEST

Nouillons. The German reaction had been immediate and violent. The Royal Scots had pulled back.

This action of the Royal Scots was interfering with the build up of the 9th Hohenstaufen Division for the counter-attack. The farmhouse at les Nouillons had been earmarked for the advance battle headquarters of the division. The entry in the war diary of Panzer Group West reads: 'Because of enemy activity on the left wing of 9th SS the counter-attack will now start at 1530 hours.'

Three miles south, across the river Odon, the Argyll and Sutherland Highlanders were holding the village of Gavrus, the western cornerstone of the defence, and the two bridges half a mile back in the valley.

The morning had been quiet. No enemy to be seen. Midday came. The sun was shining down from a clear blue sky. The only movement on this sleepy afternoon came from the birds and the bees. Major McElwee, who commanded the company in Gavrus, ordered one man from each section to mount guard. For the rest it seemed a good time to make up for lost sleep. At four o'clock the silence was brutally shattered. The whole western flank was aflame. Out of the smoke and debris that had been Gavrus came the remnants of Major McElwee's company. He had rallied them in the woods where the road drops down steeply to the bridges. It was an hour later that some battle-shattered walking wounded straggled back through the positions of the Monmouths near the Tourmauville bridge.

'What's it like then, Jock?'

'I tell ye's it's bluidy murder, man!'

North of Gavrus the Seaforth Highlanders in le Valtru were fighting for their lives. The forward company had been overrun. The company commander was dead, those men not killed had for the most part been wounded and taken prisoner. The panzers had penetrated to the crossroads, where four were ablaze in the middle of the road. Mortar fire was raining down.

A thousand yards north at Grainville, the Cameronians, too, had lost their forward company. 'Bullets streamed up every lane; the place was in flames; the wireless link with brigade had been knocked out; the telephone wires had been cut by shelling . . .' The commanding officer had gone forward to try to contact his forward troops and was missing.*

Still further north, at le Haut du Bosq, the base of the corridor, was Lieutenant Woollcombe, listening to the thunder of the guns and

* Lieutenant-Colonel Villiers had lost consciousness after being blown up on a mine.

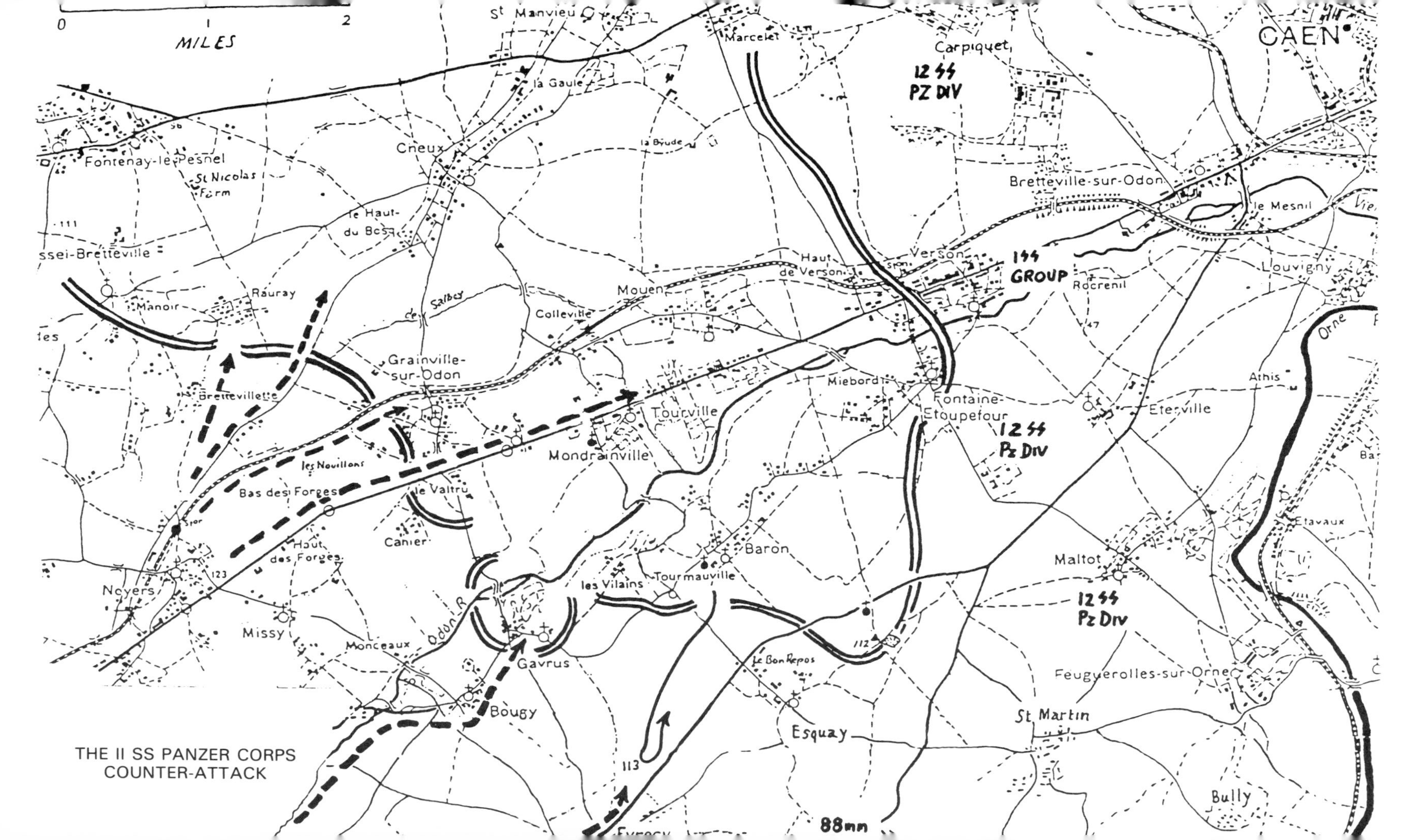

THE II SS PANZER CORPS
COUNTER-ATTACK

mortars and the intermittent rattle of machine-guns in the dust and smoke of battle half a mile down the road. There the Royal Scots were still fighting a battle of changing fortunes at Belval farm. Three Cromwells of the Northamptonshire Yeomanry had arrived and were racing backwards and forwards, turrets turning, raking the hedges and copses with long bursts of machine-gun fire. 'We blessed them, watching fascinated from our parapets, and waited for the enemy, seeing nothing and understanding less.'[4]*

It was late in the afternoon when Lieutenant Brownlie arrived in a jeep in the middle of a great flap in Cheux. The Germans were less than a mile to the west, hammering away with everything they had. Shells and mortar bombs were dropping, throwing up great fountains of earth and smoke. Vehicles were on fire. A shattering din arose from the answering fire of the British batteries in the fields around, where sweating artillerymen were slamming rounds up the spout and firing as fast as they could. Men were digging in; drivers, cooks and mechanics; anti-tank guns were being man-handled into position; Churchill tanks were everywhere, engines pulsating, moving off in groups.

The day before, Brownlie had been sent to the rear to take his turn as LOB (left out of battle). The Fifes had lost tank commanders in the action that morning, and he had now been called forward again. Coming towards him along the track was a Sherman tank. He was surprised to recognise it as the one he had handed over to Sergeant McKinnon the day before :

> McKinnon told me that it had developed a fault and that he had been sent back to workshops. He reported how the Fife and Forfars had been having a sticky time holding their positions on Hill 112. Don Hall and Freddie Craig had been wounded. The tank crew were not sorry to be leaving the battle behind.

Brownlie told the jeep driver to drive on. They went over the bare hump of hill contour 100, where so many tank men had 'bought it' on the first day of the battle. As they went down the other side towards the Caen road, Brownlie noticed how the track had suddenly become deserted. The jeep turned on to the main road :

> Driving straight towards us were three Tiger tanks and some German halftracks bristling with infantry. My driver swung the jeep

* Lieutenant Woollcombe, 6th KOSB.

round violently. A solid shot shrieked past overhead. Back down the road we pelted.

Trooper Ron Cox, like Brownlie, trying to locate and rejoin his tank squadron after repairs, also found the enemy on the main Caen road:

At a T-junction we turned left towards Caen and saw on our right German troops with their backs to us, lying in the corn and firing. We beat a hasty retreat.

Co-driver and machine-gunner John Thorpe, looking back over the Odon from a Sherman tank high on the slopes of Hill 112, could see German tanks chasing the British supply trucks:

Talk about a hunting scene! All the soft vehicles were on the run. Some were burning.

When Captain Johnny Ruffell arrived in Cheux with the food and ammunition trucks for the Monmouths he was stopped by a military policeman: 'No move south! Road under fire from enemy tanks!'

The 9th SS Hohenstaufen Division had broken through between the Cameronians in Grainville and the Seaforths in le Valtru. The supply route to the bridgehead had been cut.

There, four miles south, the Shropshires, Herefords and Monmouthshires were standing to, ready to counter-attack at Gavrus. The skies whistled and whined. The earth shuddered with the crash of each nearby shell or mortar bomb. One could hear the sound of machine-gun fire from the direction of the village, and one could still distinguish the more laboured beat of the British Brens. The Argylls were still holding out. Shermans of the Hussars came roaring across from the other side of the bridgehead to face this threat from the west. One was hit, just a dull thud, a rising cloud of dust, and the crew tumbling out of the ports and scrambling away to the hedgerow. But it didn't burst into a ball of flame.

Major Noel Bell was in a wood at the foot of Hill 112 with the transport of the Rifle Brigade:

Running down the slope came a tank sergeant. He wanted medical help. His tank had been hit by an 88 mm. The driver was dead, the co-driver had lost both his legs and the gunner had lost his sight. . . A great hail of Minnies came over. One fell just behind one of the

A Sherman of the 44th Royal Tanks taking on fuel in preparation for the advance on Evrecy.

halftracks. Shrapnel tore a great gap through the armour plate as though it were tissue paper. The lane was filled with choking, acrid smoke and dust. The back door was thrown open and everything inside was in chaos from the blast and splinters. Across the other side of Baron, an ammunition truck was ablaze. The shelling and mortaring never ceased.

On the eastern slopes of Hill 112 the Fife and Forfar tanks were engaged in a duel with 12th SS Panzers and anti-tank guns in Château de Fontaine and Eterville. On the summit the 3rd Royal Tanks supported a company of the Rifle Brigade in an advance past the calvary cross, standing where the Chemin du Duc Guillaume crosses the Evrecy road. About sixty riflemen moved forward into the little wood – it has been described as an orchard surrounded by a hedge and with a line of tall trees running through the middle. Shrapnel from shells and mortar bombs bursting in the tree-tops soon chased them out of there; they dug in on the right and left.

Two miles away, on the western side, the 44th Royal Tanks and a company of the King's Royal Rifle Corps in halftracks and carriers had pushed up the slopes of the twin summit, point 113. They dropped down into the little town of Evrecy, and met head-on with German panzers and infantry. The tank battle that followed went on most of the evening. The British tanks were forced into a fighting withdrawal under cover of smoke. Tell-tale corkscrews spiralled into the evening sky from burning tanks and vehicles. Twelve of the British tanks and two infantry halftracks lay knocked out in the hedgerows and fields.

*

At four o'clock in the afternoon a German officer had been captured near le Haut du Bosq. He was identified as from the 19th SS Panzer Grenadier Regiment, and he was carrying with him the plan of his regiment's attack towards Cheux. The 19th SS Panzer Grenadiers belonged to the 9th SS Hohenstaufen Panzer Division. A new German division had arrived.

That gave General O'Connor something to think about, but Montgomery and Dempsey, better informed through Ultra, were not surprised. They knew that there was more to come. The other division of the II SS Panzer Corps, the 10th SS Frundsberg, must also be close at hand.

*

Early reports coming back to SS Standartenfuehrer Wilhelm Bittrich, the German commander, were optimistic. Gavrus had been captured. Battlegroup Weidinger of 2nd SS was pushing troops of the 49th West Riding Division back from Rauray to protect the flank of the Hohenstaufen Division, which had overrun the forward positions of the Seaforth Highlanders at le Valtru and was reporting success at Grainville: '. . . 9th SS Panzer Regiment and the 19th SS Panzer Grenadiers capture Grainville – Next objective Cheux.'[6]

This group had broken through along the main Caen road. But the *Schwerpunkt* (main thrust) of the 9th SS counter-attack was yet to come. It was to be launched along the road leading into le Haut du Bosq, and Cheux was the objective. It had been delayed by the advance of the Royal Scots to Belval farm. The blow fell at six o'clock in the evening.

For the exhausted Royal Scots it came at the worst possible time. A relief by the Scots Fusiliers was about to begin and was causing some disorganisation. Hell suddenly descended. A massive barrage of shells and mortar bombs curtained off both sides of the road. There was confusion. German flame-throwers swept tongues of fire over the forward trenches and along the hedgerows. Clouds of black smoke billowed skywards. Bushes were burning, patches of grass were smouldering; vehicles were on fire, anti-tank guns were being shot to pieces. Smoke and fumes mixed with the dust. Panzers came crashing through hedgerows followed by groups of German infantrymen, making short runs through the mist of battle before disappearing into the smoke and confusion.

The two forward companies of the Royal Scots were overrun, and the battalion of the 49th Division across the road was crumbling. The historian of the Northamptonshire Yeomanry, which had tanks in support of the Royal Scots, states: '. . . both sides appeared to be putting down smoke, and some of our less stalwart neighbours started a back-to-the-beaches movement as though all were lost.'[21] In the confusion and excitement, the Cromwell tanks – not a type well known in the British Army – were mistaken for the enemy and were being fired at by '. . . our friends of the 8th Armoured Brigade on the opposite ridge . . .'[21]

The King's Own Scottish Borderers, in reserve, were sent forward. They moved through the falling mortar bombs, across the fields, towards the din of battle, and Lieutenant Woollcombe found himself at a company orders' group, 'crouched in the shelter of some bank, our spirits depressed by the day.' A message from Monty had arrived:

> We were, it appeared, his Nose. He had poked it outside the bridgehead. It was taking a knocking. Drawing the enemy's armoured reserves – exactly what he, Montgomery, had hoped for . . .'[4]

Monty's message had arrived, in different words, in the bridgehead itself, where Lieutenant-Colonel Churcher was addressing his officers: '1st Herefords will defend the bridge to the last man and the last round!' A similar exhortation reached the Monmouths:

> We were told the message was from Monty. That Hitler was making his big effort to wipe us out in Normandy. That this was it – we were to fight to the last man and the last round. The dramatic effect was ruined when someone in my platoon piped up with: 'But I haven't fired the first round yet, sir!' It was true. We were surrounded with raging battle, our 'C' Company had been wiped out, battalion headquarters was having a rough time in what they were calling 'death orchard', but we had yet to see a German soldier to fire at.*

Behind the Monmouths, at the base of the corridor, the crisis had reached a high point. German assault guns were at the entrance to le Haut du Bosq.

Trooper John Thorpe, who had spent the day under fire on Hill 112, and had that afternoon watched as German panzers shot up the supply routes behind them, noted in his diary:

> Warning order received: Abandon tanks after destroying gun. But no action until confirmed.

But rumour, the constant companion of crisis, must have noised abroad this extreme measure. Thorpe entered the correction:

> New orders: Retreat, taking the tanks with us. Does anyone know what's going on?

*

At eight o'clock in the evening SS Standartenfuehrer Bittrich reported that the II SS Panzer Corps was holding a line from Evrecy and Gavrus in the south, through Grainville to Rauray in the north. But although Gavrus village had been taken, 10th SS had kept south of its boundary,

* JJH – 3rd Monmouths.

the Odon, and had ignored the bridges. The 9th SS panzers and infantry that had infiltrated along the main Caen road were being driven back, counter-attacked by the British tanks that O'Connor had kept for that purpose.

*

It was spitting with rain and the evening was set for decline when SS Obergrupppenfuehrer Paul Hausser, still commanding in Normandy in the absence of Rommel, came through on the telephone to exhort Bittrich to greater effort:

> The II SS Panzer Corps counter-attack presents *the* big opportunity. The *Schwerpunkt* is to be kept on the left with Cheux as the main objective.[17]

But Bittrich had bad news. Success was turning sour. His panzers and infantry were being forced back by the weight of the British artillery. And there was worse. The second assault wave, the Panther battalion and the motorised grenadiers, had been about to leave their concentration area in the woods at Bas des Forges, when British bombers had appeared in the skies above and bombed them:

> The bombs rained down. They tore at the earth. They snapped the tree trunks like matchsticks, threw armoured vehicles into the air, ripped off the tracks and even the armour plate.[6]

The killed and wounded numbered sixty. Twenty percent of the infantry halftracks were out of action. The 9th SS Hohenstaufen battle headquarters at nearby les Nouillons had also been caught in the attack. The survivors were dazed and disorganised. The second wave of assault troops that was to push the counter-attack through to Cheux failed to get off the start-line.

At a time when requests by the Army for air support were producing comments like: 'The Army does not seem prepared to fight its own battles',* Montgomery had applied through Eisenhower to Bomber Command for help. That he had been prepared to go, cap in hand, to those who at that moment were undermining his leadership at supreme headquarters, was a measure of his concern for the outcome of this battle.

At ten o'clock the British tanks received the order to withdraw across the Odon. 'It seemed a pity to be giving up ground so hardly won . . .'

* Attributed to Air Marshal Coningham.

wrote the historian of the 23rd Hussars. The order to abandon Hill 112 came as a shock. Despite the loss of some hundred tanks and four hundred men of tank crew, the general feeling was that a further sweep south across the Odon was 'well within its powers'. Replacements had been arriving to fill the gaps, tanks had been repaired or replaced, and morale was high. However, by nightfall, tanks were beginning to edge their way down the steep winding road to the Tourmauville bridge. In a dark night that was to teem with rain two hundred tanks would have to make that perilous journey without lights.

Coming in the opposite direction was Lieutenant Brownlie, who had joined up with the supply vehicles of the Fife and Forfar Yeomanry. Late in the evening the route had at last been declared free of enemy interference:

> The track was crammed with vehicles, and there was much enemy shelling. The situation worsened with the growing darkness. It was night when we reached the bridge. Tanks were going past us in the opposite direction. It could only mean that one of the regiments was being withdrawn. We hardly moved. A shell fell and killed some men nearby. More shells. We couldn't go on. With difficulty we turned the trucks round. Then we heard that our own tanks were being withdrawn. The salient had become a seething mass of men and vehicles; the narrow roads and tracks were nose to tail with tanks, trucks and guns. The confusion was incredible. There was chaos on the crossroads outside Cheux, where a truck had overturned and was blocking the way.

At le Haut du Bosq the battle had tailed off into an uneasy silence of suspense. Daylight was already fading when Cromwell tanks of the Northamptonshire Yeomanry were ordered to sweep the area, contact Scottish infantry somewhere further forward, and boost morale by staying with them for the night. A sudden bout of shelling killed and wounded some of the tank crew and delayed the start.

One group moved forward into the dark and found the Scotsmen holding Belval farm. At midnight a second group came up on the wireless net with the information that it was lost, was surrounded by the enemy and was under attack. It requested permission to withdraw. Permission was refused. A second request was likewise rejected. At one o'clock the wireless went dead. Seven tanks and thirty-five crewmen were missing.*

* It was later established that twenty-seven had been killed.

CHAPTER NINE

The End of Epsom

30th June 1944

An hour before dawn, the last of the 11th Armoured Division troops on Hill 112, a company of the 8th Rifle Brigade, withdrew down the slopes in the dark and followed the tanks over the Tourmauville bridge. The British had given up Hill 112. Left behind at the foot of the hill was the infantry. Their task was to hold on to the much reduced bridgehead over the Odon. With their anti-tank guns and the support of the artillery, they were to repel the onslaught that must surely come soon from the high ground just abandoned.

As the Rifle Brigade's halftracks and carriers were driving in the half-light of dawn back down the Scottish corridor, so the sky above Hill 112 filled with the wail, the whine and the whistle of Moaning Minnies and shells. The mortars of two Werfer brigades and the guns of two artillery divisions were softening up the summit for a full-scale German attack. The top of the hill disappeared in great clouds of dust and smoke; the earth trembled with crashes and bangs. By half-past-seven that morning the hill was back in German hands.

German observation posts were looking down on the British positions in the valley of the Odon below and could see right back over the Epsom battlefield. They were directing the fire of the German artillery and those 'particularly powerful weapons' – the words are those of the war diary of the OKW* – the Moaning Minnies of the 7th and 8th Werfer Brigades. 'Death Valley' was about to earn its name.

During the night, troops of the 53rd Welsh Division, newly arrived from England, had moved into the area of le Mesnil Patry – quickly

* OKW — Oberkommando der Wehrmacht (High Command of the German Armed Forces).

corrupted to 'mess in the pantry'. It was a village on the start-line of the opening Epsom battle and was now in what was considered a rear area. At nine o'clock the commanding officer assembled his officers to give orders for a take-over that night from a battalion of the 15th Scottish. They were suddenly plastered by shell fire; two men were killed and six were wounded. The Welsh Guards, also new from England, lost their commanding officer and second-in-command, both killed, when a concentration of Minnies fell on them just south of Cheux. The engineers lost four officers while building a second crossing over the Odon, and Major General Thomas, commander of the 43rd Wessex Division, was forced to run for shelter when his staff car came under accurate bombardment.

Tourville was a particularly hot spot. For two days the 3rd Monmouths had been losing men there. When the squirl of the bagpipes heralded the Gordons, marching west in long files towards the open ground west of the château, the Welshmen could hardly believe their eyes and ears. An attempt was made to stop them. The Gordons would have none of it. As they moved across the open field a crescendo of Minnies drowned out the sound of the pipes. The Minnies screamed down. The Gordons scattered. A series of deafening explosions threw up fountains of earth and stones. Casualties were heavy. The Gordons got the message. They moved back into Tourville, where they remained under 'continual mortaring until their relief on the night of the 1st July. It was to be a costly twenty-four hours.'[20]

General O'Connor met his commanders at eleven o'clock in the morning. Epsom was over. Now they must hold on to what they had won. The German counter-attack of the previous day was only a preliminary. A source of reliable information was warning that a much more powerful counter-blow was on the way. The tanks were being held at the base of the salient in readiness to counter the next enemy move. The attack would come in again from the west. The blow might fall at any moment.

With hindsight one realises that the 'source of reliable information' was Ultra, and that the withdrawal of the tanks from the bridgehead had been prompted by Montgomery. The 9th SS Hohenstaufen Panzer Division had been identified as the counter-attacking force the previous day. But where was the 10th SS Frundsberg Division? It was the second of the two panzer divisions with the II SS Panzer Corps, which had been arriving from Russia.

Ultra had also told Montgomery of the movement to Normandy of two other SS Panzer divisions. Units of one, the 2nd SS Das Reich

Division, were under command of 9th SS, and the mass of the division was assembled not far away at Caumont. Elements of the 1st SS Adolf Hitler Division had also been identified on the battlefield, and the mass of that division must be lurking close at hand.

The British were soon to learn of the presence of the 10th SS Frundsberg Division. It was on top of Hill 112. It was this division that had driven the Argyll and Sutherland Highlanders out of Gavrus the day before, and had forced the 44th Royal Tanks to retreat with heavy losses from Evrecy. At dawn it had advanced up the slopes of Hill 112 from the south, while panzers and infantry of the Hitler Youth Division had attacked from Maltot in the east. The 10th SS Frundsberg Division was fighting south of the Odon river, the 9th SS Hohenstaufen north of it.

In the command posts of the enemy there was on this morning much discussion and despondency at the failure of the two counter-attacking divisions to cut through the salient and bring about the destruction of the British VIII Corps. The reports from 9th SS and Battlegroup Weidinger (2nd SS) showed that morale had taken a hard knock.

Never before had the Waffen SS troops met such concentrated and accurate artillery defensive fire. Never before had they experienced such domination of the skies by the enemy. Never before had they been under the fire of heavy naval guns. A report sent in by Battlegroup Weidinger mentioned a direct hit on a command post that had killed all ten occupants. Telephone wires had everywhere been cut, and no sooner were they repaired than they were cut again. Scarcely a linesman, runner or liaison officer had survived the battle unwounded. Loss of communications had brought doubt and uncertainty. Tight control of the battle had been impossible. The commander of one panzer grenadier regiment had found it necessary to send the following message to his signallers: 'Field of fire always takes priority over cover from fire – that applies to wireless operators, too!' Signallers had been staying off the air, fearing to be pinpointed and given as a target to the British artillery. The defensive artillery never let up as soon as it had latched on to something to fire at. The infantry had been pinned to the ground, unable to move, unable to bring its firepower to bear.

The 10th SS, operating against the bridgehead, had also had difficulties. Having captured Gavrus, they were then forced out by the weight of the British artillery fire that descended on the village. They dug in hard south, leaving Gavrus deserted in 'no man's land' for the night. The group advancing to take Hill 112 was halted by the kind of 'cock up' that the British soldiers thought could only happen to them. Luftwaffe flak gunners in the village of Avenay mistook the Germans for a British force and stopped them with the devastating fire of their 88 mm guns.

The telephone lines connecting the German command posts were busy all morning. Dietrich of the 1st SS Panzer Corps spoke to General Geyr von Schweppenburg of Panzer Group West. He was against continuing the counter-attack : the situation was very difficult. Schweppenburg passed that information on to Hausser and drew particular attention to the damage being done by the British naval guns, in which 'even the attacks of the II SS Panzer Corps had come to nothing'. Bittrich, the commander of the II SS Panzer Corps and the man fighting the battle, had already decided on a course of action. He would cut out the British artillery observation officers in their spotter planes hovering above the battle, and in their posts of vantage on the ground. He would attack at night.

*

The 15th Scottish had carried the main weight of the Epsom battles. They had lost over two thousand five hundred men. That was an eighteen percent casualty rate for the division; but eighty percent of the losses had been suffered by the combat soldiers of the rifle companies: they were down to half strength and below. These were the

SS Oberfuehrer Harmel (left), commander of the 10th SS Frundsberg Division, interrogating the crew of a British tank that has been knocked out.

men who were holding the dangerous western flank of the corridor. But the 53rd Welsh Division had arrived from England, and over the next three nights would take over the Scottish positions. The infantry brigade of the Guards Armoured Division had also arrived, and was under command of the Wessex Division on the eastern side of the corridor.

The base of the Corridor was now very strong. The once lonely plain behind Cheux was thick with guns. Everywhere gunners were toiling in the mud and the sticky June heat. Command posts had been dug into the sides of the ditches. With guns firing all round them, signallers were unravelling messages and orders from a background babble of voices. But in this area, where the 9th SS Hohenstaufen Division had attacked with such fierce determination the day before, there was no sign of the onslaught being renewed.

South of the river, however, 10th SS, morale heightened at finding that the British had abandoned Hill 112, was probing aggressively down the hill towards the bridgehead, testing the British defences and working its way forward in preparation for the assault that would wipe out the bridgehead that night.

It struck first at the weakest point, the Argyll and Sutherland Highlanders, isolated at the Gavrus bridges. Their headquarters, on the northern bank of the Odon, was pin-pointed by enemy artillery and mortars and given the full treatment. Trucks went up in flames; the wireless link with the supporting artillery 'went for a Burton', and communications with the main body of the battalion holding out across the river were cut. Agitated survivors filtered back into Tourville Brigade gave the order to withdraw. Anti-tank guns, tanks and a machine-gun company were sent along the northern bank to control the withdrawal. The commanding officer was missing. He had gone on foot to cross the river and pass the order on to those on the other side. He had not returned and there was still no contact.

When the withdrawal order did get through, passed on orally by a young tank officer through two junior infantry officers, the commander, Major McElwee, rejected it. His orders were to fight on. He would do just that. He would accept only a written order, not one passed on by word of mouth. The frustration of one officer involved in this incident exploded: 'For God's sake get out of this cursed wood and don't be so obstinate!' But McElwee was not to be moved.

It was nine o'clock in the evening when an officer from brigade finally got through with the written authority that Major McElwee's honour demanded: 'We withdrew in good order with two hundred

7th Royal Tank Regiment.

'Lancasters of Bomber Command were droning past overhead.'

Panzer grenadiers.

and three men – we even brought the two anti-tank guns out with us.'

At the Tourmauville bridge Lieutenant-Colonel Jack Churcher was receiving reports from his patrols of German armour and infantry massing for an attack. Together with the commanding officer of the Ayrshire Yeomanry field artillery he prepared the three defensive artillery barrages code-named Dorothy, Dainty and Duchess. As the 10th SS attack moved in, regiment after regiment of guns, field, medium and heavy, was switched in to thicken up the barrage. The 10th SS grenadiers and assault guns withered away under the weight of over fifteen thousand shells.

*

At Belval farm, just off the road leading into le Haut du Bosq and Cheux, that scene of fierce battle the day before, the King's Own Scottish Borderers had taken over. Lieutenant Woollcombe's platoon was digging in beneath the tall hedges of the orchard: 'All the khaki figures in the fields below straightened up from their shovels, tilted their helmets off their brows, and smiled as if a tonic had been administered.'[4]

Lancasters of Bomber Command were droning past overhead. For the second night running Montgomery had brought in the 'heavies'. The little town of Villers-Bocage, clustered round a road junction a few miles away, was about to be destroyed. The enemy had on this day restricted himself to probing attacks to test the defence and to gain a good start-line for the counter-attack that was to go in under cover of darkness. The effectiveness of the German artillery and mortar fire can be judged from the thousand plus casualties suffered by VIII Corps during the twenty-four hours: one hundred and fifty-four men had been killed, and two hundred and forty-two were missing.

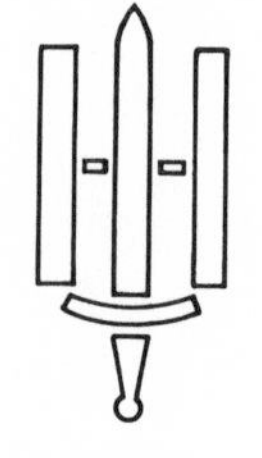

9 SS 'H' Pz DIV

10 SS 'F' Pz DIV

CHAPTER TEN

Here comes that bloody man the gunner, thank God![22]

1st July 1944

It had started just before one o'clock in the morning. Calls in English came from the silent darkness of 'no man's land', from the fields of stubble and corn in front of the positions of the Shropshires at Baron : 'Tommy – I can see you !' – 'Tommy – we are coming !' Jumpy sentries let loose with rifle and machine-gun, firing towards the voices in the night. Sleeping men were quickly aroused. All were standing-to when the silence was shattered by the shrieks and screams of mortar bombs and shells hurtling down towards them.

The Monmouths had a grandstand view from the high ground across the river Odon :

> It was the sergeant who jerked me out of deep sleep into a night of bangs and crashes and flashing light. In the bridgehead across the river the Herefords and Shropshires were getting a pasting. Explosive flashes darted rapidly about in the valley below; strings of tracer curved slowly and gracefully away into extinction; flames flickered in the darkness; and Very lights hung seemingly motionless over the valley. The noise was deafening. How, I wondered, could anyone survive down there.*

It was Dainty, Dorothy and Duchess, the three pre-arranged defensive fire tasks, to the rescue again. They came howling through the night from the guns of twelve regiments of artillery.

Dug in across the Odon was Sergeant Frank Moppett of the Herefords :

> It went on for hours, and we suffered mentally as much as the Germans – the constant scream of shells overhead, the crash of

* JJH – 3rd Monmouths.

Dainty, Dorothy and Duchess to the rescue. A 4.5 inch medium gun in action at night.

> German shells exploding amongst us. And we were being hit by our own shells falling short.

The mortars of the Shropshires, behind the church at Baron, came under rifle and machine-gun fire. German infantry had infiltrated. The field exploded into brilliant light. A mortar pit had received a direct hit from a phosphorus bomb. Two crew members were burned. 'Sergeant Jack Morris was by my side one minute and prostrate the next with a shrapnel hole in the cheek. Big Percy Davies helped Sergeant Baker to recover the mortar sights . . .'[23]* The mortar positions had to be abandoned.

The sound of rifle and machine-gun fire from the forward platoons showed that they were in direct contact with the enemy. Vehicles at battalion headquarters had been hit. Shrapnel thrown down from the trees was causing casualties. The wireless halftrack, the vital link with brigade and with the companies fighting the battle, was rocking and heaving from near misses. Shell splinters were tearing through the soft, upper part of the roof. The adjutant and signallers inside were putting through urgent calls for yet more fire from Dainty, Duchess and Dorothy. That the company wireless truck had disappeared in a mass of flames could not destroy the urbanity of Corporal Ralph; he reported to the company commander: 'Please sir, the wireless is out of action.'

Darkness brings fear and uncertainty. The heavy bombardment restricted movement, brought tension and sapped resistance. No one knew quite what was happening. But with some fire coming from the rear and the flanks, it was certain that some of the enemy were amongst them. The terrible night turned into a silent dawn. The hunt for the intruders started. They proved to be heavily armed and determined. In clashes that morning the Shropshires killed twenty-five and took ten prisoner. Many German dead lay in the cornfields where the Shropshires picked up twenty-three German machine-guns from a litter of abandoned equipment.

Sergeant Moppett of the Herefords was sent forward along the Esquay road, up the slope of Hill 112. His task was to assess the effect of the British artillery fire:

> Arriving at what I thought was the crest, I ordered the men to dismount. We went forward on foot. It was a false crest. The real one was a hundred yards further on. All round was quiet. The sun shone

* Sergeant Langford, 4th KSLI.

in a blue sky. We could forget the war was on. Then I saw the turret of a tank on our left. I crawled through the corn with Lance-Corporal Morten. It was knocked-out. Behind were several more. We returned to the road and moved over the crest. Then I realised why the Germans wanted the hill. You could see for miles – over to Esquay and on to Evrecy and right over the Orne river. Everything was still quiet.

We moved on. Carnage. Dead Germans everywhere. Literally in piles amongst the wheat. There were seven or eight knocked-out tanks. At the side of the road we found a row of wounded Germans. They had received some first-aid treatment and then been left for the night. The first man was blond, blue eyes looking into mine. His right hand was blown off and he was leaning his head on the stump. '*Wasser – Wasser*', was all he said. Next to them was the remains of a headquarters. I collected some marked maps. The platoon commander, Captain Barnaby, had come forward.

As we were discussing the maps, my look-out shouted: 'Sarge! Steel helmets in the corn!' On our right about a hundred yards away, we could see German helmets moving. All hell let loose. From Esquay, straight up the road, and from both sides came Spandau fire. Captain Barnaby was hit with the first burst. I got him into a carrier and sent him back to the RAP.* My Bren guns were answering as best they could. I shouted for the carrier with the two inch mortar and the Vickers gun. It slewed round to give us some cover. I called for everyone to mount. Corporal Curtis was killed instantly, shot through the head as he fell into the carrier. I jumped on to the sloping front and we withdrew back over the crest. Then I pulled into a field and got the Brens into position in case we were followed. A mortar bomb exploded amongst us. Lance-Corporal Morten had shrapnel in the thigh and the corporal was wounded in the face; one of the drivers was blinded.

Back in the 'safety' of the Herefords' position, Sergeant Moppett lost another driver, who was hit in the head by shrapnel. Captain Barnaby died of his wounds.

I had a moment of panic. In my first engagement I had lost my platoon commander, a corporal, a lance-corporal and two drivers. After four years of training together for the war, half my section had gone in a couple of hours. How long would we last, I wondered.

* Regimental Aid Post.

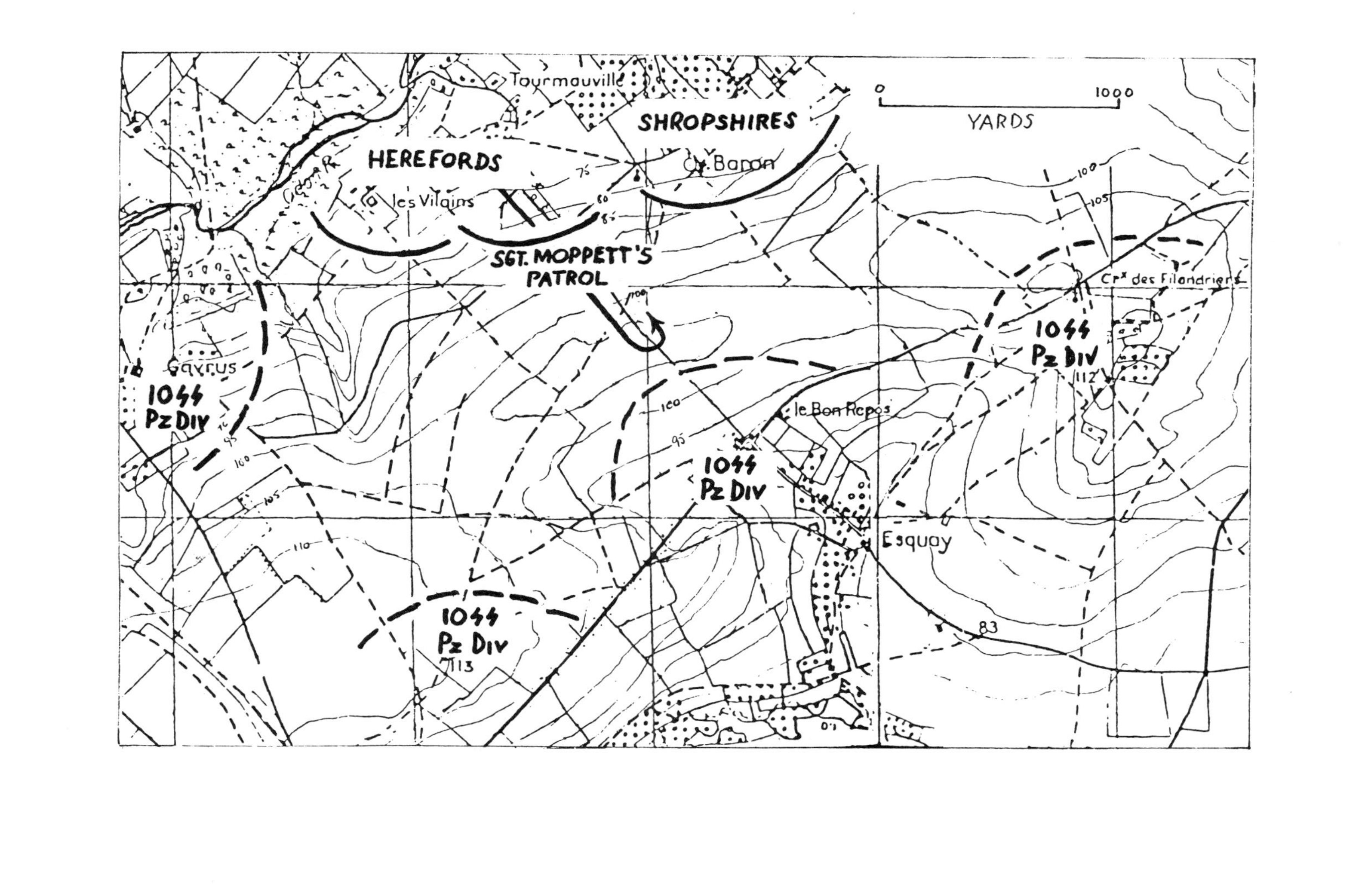

Tourmauville
SHROPSHIRES
0
1000
YARDS
HEREFORDS
Baron
les Vilains
SGT. MOPPETT'S
PATROL
Crx des Filondriers
1044
Pz DIV
112
Gavrus
1044
Pz DIV
le Bon Repos
1044
Pz DIV
Esquay
1044
Pz DIV
113
83

*

'Hello, Jig Able Baker – Hello, Jig Able Baker – Much enemy movement in front of me – Over.'

'Speak up – I can't hear.'

'I can't talk loudly – the enemy is too close.'

'Do you want the defensive fire task?'

'Yes – DF 109.'[24]

A company of the King's Own Scottish Borderers was dug in on the left-hand side of the road leading to that hot spot, le Haut du Bosq. It was an hour past midnight. Sergeant Murray had just returned from patrol with a report of Germans assembling in numbers just down the road.

DF 109 came whistling through the night sky to lay a carpet of shells in front of the company positions. The answer came back almost immediately; a great weight of shells and bombs on Belval farm, the battalion headquarters. Two men were killed. Then silence crept back again to make the sentries nervous. All day they had been waiting for the Germans to renew their counter-attack. Day had turned into night. The Scotsmen were standing to, half of them awake and watching at all times.

Throughout the night the two sides were lined up a few hundred yards apart, weapons at the ready. The German unit commanders had gathered at the headquarters of the Der Fuehrer Regiment and were waiting for the order that would set the night alight. It didn't come. SS Obersturmfuehrer Woith, the officer entrusted with the order, had run into artillery fire on the way and been severely wounded. The telephone lines were broken: there was strict wireless silence. It was dawn by the time a second messenger got through.

Lieutenant Woollcombe woke up to hear someone shouting: 'Stand to! – Get the men standing to!' It was his company commander. He walked past, rifle in hand, binoculars dangling from his neck. There had been little sleep; two hours on, two hours off throughout the night.

There is no glory in modern war. No bugles blowing and no flags flying. Just little groups of tired men in holes in the ground; trying to stay alive.

Enemy shells were falling thickly now. The British artillery was joining in. Soon the din was so great that one had to shout to make oneself heard. The enemy, it seems, was trying to advance along the road. That was somewhere in front, about two hundred yards away. One couldn't see for the smoke. No enemy here. But there was firing down there on the road. Somebody said there were German tanks and flame throwers.

Then at half-past-nine the shelling stopped. There was an uncertain calm. 'What's the griff? Has Jerry given up then?' Nobody knew.

At half-past-ten the heavens again filled with whines and whistles; the fields shuddered with the falling missiles.

Close to the hedge, in the field on the roadside was an anti-tank gun. Private Crozier and Private Brown lay dead nearby. Corporal Wallace had been wounded. Only Captain Elliot was still there to fire the gun. There was a blinding flash. He was thrown out of the gun pit by the explosion. He, too, was wounded.

Back at Belval farm, in the orchard, Lieutenant Woollcombe was still watching from his trencch. A figure was running towards the farm from the roadside:

> It stumbled through our positions; a Jock from some other company, and quite young. Some of us called to him, but he was out of his wits. He passed on, sobbing in gulps, the tears streaking the dirt and sweat on his face – making for he knew not where. And we saw two or three more figures in khaki moving back in disorder across the field, to disappear in a wood behind us. Then two men with a different badge on their shoulders arrived among us, who came from the battalion across the road, the left flank battalion of the other corps, whose front had disintegrated. Quietly the refugees stayed to fight with us . . . A little later a small column of some twenty men under an officer . . . wended their way into our area, and threw themselves on their backs among our trenches, staring apathetically upwards. They came from 'C' Company . . . [4]

And so it came about that Woollcombe was called to attend an order group, a few anxious men gathered in the corner of a field. A machine-gun was firing not far away. Counter-attack! That was the order now. A counter-attack to support what was left of that company down on the road. 'What about the German tanks?' Well they didn't matter. This, you see, was an order from the brigadier himself.

The men climbed out of their trenches. They moved half-crouching along the hedgerow. Shells were falling. There was a long halt. The men pressed themselves into the comforting grass. Just ahead in that confusion of smoke and shell fire was the country road. The noise was deafening. The company commander had gone forward on reconnaissance. He didn't come back. When the stretcher-bearers found him, '. . . he told them to leave him and look after the men who were coming back from all directions'.[24]

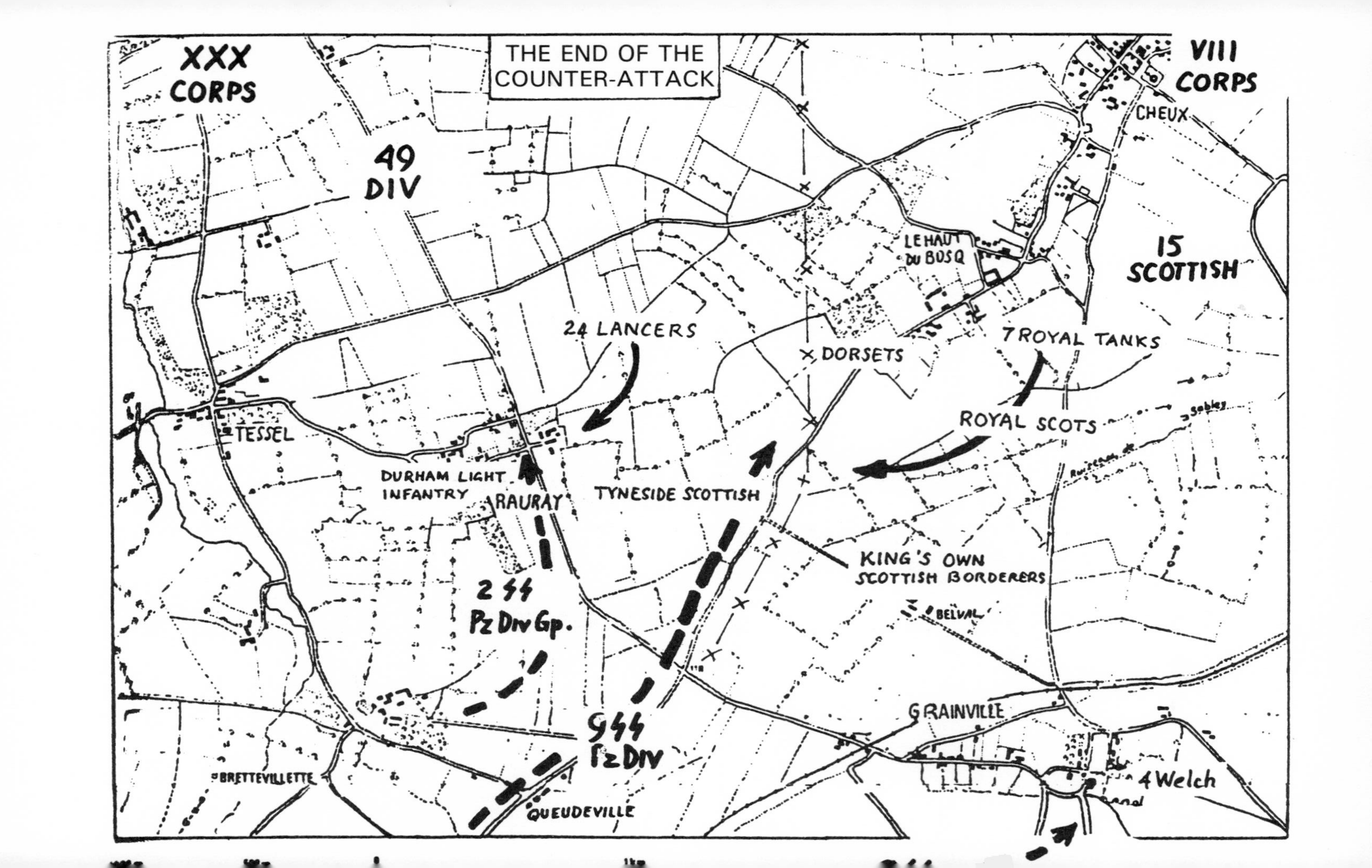
THE END OF THE
COUNTER-ATTACK
XXX
CORPS
VIII
CORPS
CHEUX
49
DIV
15
SCOTTISH
LE HAUT
DU BOSQ
24 LANCERS
7 ROYAL TANKS
DORSETS
ROYAL SCOTS
TESSEL
DURHAM LIGHT
INFANTRY
RAURAY
TYNESIDE SCOTTISH
KING'S OWN
SCOTTISH BORDERERS
BELVAL
2 SS
Pz Div Gp.
9 SS
Pz DIV
GRAINVILLE
4 Welch
BRETTEVILLETTE
QUEUDEVILLE

Herbert Fuerbringer was eighteen years old, a member of a heavy machine-gun team of four men with the 19th SS Panzer Grenadier Regiment (9th SS). The gun was in position facing the Scotsmen at Belval farm. Fuerbringer was sent back to bring up more ammunition :

> I was told it was stored in the sacristy of the church at Grainville, the only building strong enough to withstand the artillery fire. I was on my way back when the British artillery fire suddenly increased. I ran, looking for shelter. I came to a shattered motorcycle. Lying nearby with waxen face was Rudi Klinger, our company despatch rider. He had been bringing ammunition forward in the sidecar and had received a direct hit. As I looked I was overcome with horror. The head was almost severed from the body, just hanging on by a few bits of muscle and skin. The shells were dropping further back so I made a run for the machine-gun position. But down they came again – worse than before. I lay flattened in the bottom of the road-side ditch. The shells had come howling down right into the machine-gun post.

Fuerbringer's three comrades were killed; the machine-gun was torn from its mounting; the bent barrel was pointed skywards. A shaken and dazed Fuerbringer wandered back into the ruins of Grainville looking for his company headquarters. It had moved.

The night before, the 53rd Welsh Division, just landed in Normandy, had been rushed forward to relieve the remnants of the hard-pressed and battle-weary Scotsmen. In the black night – it had started to rain again – the Welshmen stumbled in long files over the fields. The 5th Welch lost fifty men from shell fire even before they had arrived at le Valtru to relieve the Seaforth Highlanders. The 4th Welch took over from the Cameronians near Grainville. With the dawn came the inferno. 'Multi-barrelled mortars with their loud screech, phosphorus shells, heavy guns, light guns, air bursts, mortars and spandau machine-guns – all were hurling death and destruction.'[36] Within five minutes of his arrival the new commanding officer, his second-in-command and adjutant had to be rescued from the debris of a command post that had received a direct hit. A panzer lumbered through the hedge and was knocked out. Panzer grenadiers overran the forward positions. There was confusion. The Welshmen had been thrown into terrifying reality. But by the afternoon the German attack was petering out. 'The men shook the dust from their hair and wiped the sweat from their faces and – laughed.'[36]

The turning point had come when Captain Shaw, perched high in the roof of Belval farm, had spotted German panzers and infantry forming up near Queudeville to attack. He got every gun in VIII Corps switched on to them. This German force was seen also by an artillery observer of the 49th West Riding Division in Rauray, and he had brought down every gun in XXX Corps. No wonder an officer of the 9th SS Hohenstaufen Division finished his battle report with a quotation from Dante : '. . . abandon hope all ye who enter here!'

In the evening men of the King's Own Scottish Borders were able once again to occupy the positions that had been lost on the side of the road. They found the hulks of three knocked-out panzers and the bodies of their own and the German dead. Across the road, in the area of the 49th West Riding Division, the Tyneside Scottish and Durham Light Infantry had lost between them in the day's fighting four hundred men. Battlegroup Weidinger (2nd SS) fought its way forward right into the outskirts of Rauray. They were counter-attacked by tanks of the 24th Lancers, and withdrew under heavy pressure, being forced to leave behind their wounded, who were taken prisoner. The West Riding Division claimed to have knocked out thirty enemy tanks.

The Scottish infantry had been in action for six days. During that time many had been unable to wash or shave or take their boots off. For six nights they had scarcely slept. Battalion casualties ranged from the two hundred of the King's Own Scottish Borderers to over three hundred of the Seaforth Highlanders.

They had entered the battle as soldiers untested by combat, they would leave it as war-scarred veterans. 'The losses in my company were very heavy, and the sad thing about it was that most of them came from the same district, even the same village.'[8]*

The battle report of the 9th SS Hohenstaufen Division describes the massed effect of the British artillery as reminiscent of the barrages of the First World War, both in the weight of shells and the duration of the bombardment. It is at pains to point out that this and this alone had brought about the failure to achieve the objectives. It stresses the very heavy losses. In three days of battle the Hohenstaufen Division had suffered 1,145 casualties, and Battlegroup Weidinger 636. Thirty-two panzers and assault guns, eleven anti-tank guns and seven infantry guns had been knocked out, and there were heavy losses in mortars, machine-guns and wireless equipment.

* Captain Hume, Royal Scots.

ıe top two illustrations show e battlefield on the Rauray ad, where the 49th West ding Division had been in rce combat with Battle-oup Weidinger (2nd SS) pported by Tiger tanks of e 1 SS Panzer Corps.

op) The rolled-up gas cape entifies the dead man as itish; on the right is the two-ch mortar he has been rrying. The knocked-out nk is a Tiger.

entre) The panzer grenadier ng dead in the roadway has en runover by a tank. The otorcycle belongs to the itish despatch rider on the ht. The knocked-out tank on e crest is a Tiger.

ıerman tanks at harbour in orchard. The grave is that a panzer grenadier of the tler Youth Division.

Details of the losses of the 10th SS Frundsberg Division did not survive the war; the historian of the II SS Panzer Corps considers that they were similar to those of the Hohenstaufen Division.

The Hitler Youth Division had lost 1,240 men in killed, wounded and missing: heavy casualties when one bears in mind that a part of the division further east in defence of Caen was not involved.

The 43rd Wessex Division, uninvolved in the opening battle and later in defence on the less active eastern side of the corridor, had suffered only light casualties. Its big battle, and horrific losses on Hill 112, were still ten days away. The British 11th Armoured Division had gone into action with 12,050 men and lost a thousand. Heaviest casualties were in the tank units, where losses in tank crew reached thirty-three percent. But by far the heaviest burden had been carried by the 15th Scottish Division, with 2,720 casualties. For a division that had entered the battle with 15,005 men that does not seem a crippling loss; but in terms of fighting men, the men who face the enemy with rifles, machine-guns and anti-tank guns, who suffer ninety percent of all casualties, it meant that for every ten men who went into the battle only five came out. Regimental esprit, the mutual trust of men in the fighting platoons, carefully built up in years of training, would have a struggle to survive.

One category of battle casualty does not appear in the campaign histories, yet no unit, regular, volunteer or conscript, élitist para-commando, footslogger or tanker, is without those who break down under the strain of modern warfare. Some will collapse in the first twenty-four hours; others will fight bravely for weeks, before being overwhelmed by the loss of friends and by the odds piling up against them, and there are those who will see the whole campaign to the end with no apparent sign of wear. But they will not be many, for most will long before that be carried off the battlefield on a stretcher or finish in a grave. Of the former, some will return, nervous system restocked during the period of recovery.

Battle is a great leveller. Failure of the nervous system is no respecter of rank. There are always surprises, like the brigadier who at the start of Epsom had to be evacuated; he was a veteran of that other war. The behaviour of one infantry battalion commander under fire was so alarming that his subordinate company commanders contrived his removal with the aid of the medical officer. Then there was the bright young captain, an officer of promise until he tried to board a landing craft to get back to England. His fellow officers knew only that he had disappeared. It was much later that they learned that he had been sent back to the UK under medical care, where he became an instructor – no doubt on the strength of his experience. More surprising is that this officer was given, later, a commission in the regular army. A surprise, too, was the regimental sergeant major, a soldier holding an award for gallantry, who lasted just nine days.

Then there was Lieutenant 'Pinchy-Boots'. The death of a friend in the first twenty-four hours of battle shattered what little reserve of courage he had. Faced with the sight of enemy panzers and infantry about to attack, he not only panicked himself but spread it to those around him. He led his men in a mini-retreat to the beaches. They went only about a hundred yards. A burly major of engineers confronted them in the narrow country lane: 'And where do you think you're going?' 'Pinchy-Boots', sensing trouble, had already made himself scarce. It was a corporal who faced the major's wrath. 'Well, sir, I don't know where we're going, but I know it's in this direction.' 'That's what you think!' bawled the major. 'Get back to your trenches!' The men turned round, confidence restored, and did as they were ordered. All of which seems to prove the old army adage that there are no bad men, only bad officers. Pinchy-Boots disappeared, an exit no doubt assisted by the medical officer. They were always helpful and understanding. 'Well, you didn't want him hanging around, did you?'

Soldiers who broke down were often 'carried' by their mates until an incident revealed the true situation. A self-inflicted wound to the hand or foot brought a quick departure, and there were members of tank crews who contrived to trap a foot and break it whilst jumping from the tank: a prospect that seemed to many to require more courage than facing up to battle. Genuine wounds and injuries of this kind could prove embarrassing, particularly at a later stage in the campaign, when special reports were required on those who suffered them.

But mental breakdown affected only an insignificant minority during the Epsom battles. That is what one would expect of units that had been subjected to hard training and constant vetting. That such cases did occur shows how difficult it is to predict the behaviour of a soldier facing battle for the first time. In battles which produced from both sides some of the heaviest artillery and mortar bombardments of the war one can only wonder at the courage and steadfastness of all those men who resolutely stood their ground.

*

Field-Marshal von Rundstedt had returned from the interview with Hitler in Berchtesgaden. He had had plenty of time to brood on it.

There was irritation at his failure to put over to Hitler his opinion that Germany had already lost the war; there was irritation at being kept waiting in Hitler's ante-room; and irritation at not being invited to dine at the Fuehrer's table. To this was now added the information of the failure of the II SS Panzer Corps counter-attack. News of that had already reached Hitler. Field-Marshal Keitel, Chief of the German High Command, immediately put through a high priority call to von Rundstedt. There was a note of despair in his voice :

> What shall we do? What shall we do?
> Make peace, you idiots! What else can you do?

Von Rundstedt's reply was passed on to Hitler. For him it was one more example of the defeatism of his generals. Had he not been saying that they were responsible for the recent set-backs?

On von Rundstedt's desk, awaiting his return, was a report from General Geyr von Schweppenburg, commander of Panzer Group West. In it he outlined the consequences of the failure of the German counter-attack and the fall of Cherbourg :

> A drive to the beaches followed by the destruction of the Allied armies was no longer a reality. Neither was a policy of obstinate defence, for that would leave the initiative with Montgomery. On the other hand, limited withdrawals, a straightening of the front, which would take the battle out of the range of the British naval guns, would give the German panzer commanders the chance to use their skill and their experience of mobile warfare. Only in that way could the German Army hope to regain something of the initiative.

The report had been approved by both SS Obergruppenfuehrer Hausser, commander of the German Seventh Army, and Field-Marshal Rommel, who had added a request for permission to evacuate Caen as a first step to shortening the front.

In the discussions that followed, Rommel's chief of staff stated that if the front were not shortened within a few days then 9th, 10th, 12th SS Panzer Divisions and the Panzer Lehr Division would become so burnt out that they would no longer be fit for action.

The report was forwarded to Hitler. His reaction was immediate. He sent a personal adjutant to conduct an examination on the spot. He carried with him the award of the Knight's Cross of the Iron Cross with Oakleaves, which was to be presented to Field-Marshal von

Rundstedt together with a letter from the Fuehrer congratulating him and accepting his 'resignation' on health grounds.

General Geyr von Schweppenburg became the scapegoat. He was dismissed, but not before he had telephoned the commanders of the I SS and II SS Panzer Corps telling them not to conceal in any way the extent of the set-back and seriousness of the losses suffered in the counter-attack.

For the soldiers who had fought the battle with bravery Hitler had only bitter complaint: they had, he said, lacked commitment to the cause; they were without experience and inadequately trained. With the following order of the day he brought the German counter-attack to an end:

> The Fuehrer has decided:
> The present position must be held. Any further attempt to break out by the enemy must be met with determined defence or counter-attack.[11]*

During a farewell visit to Rommel's headquarters, von Rudstedt expressed his relief that he would not be one of the military leaders to experience the coming catastrophe. How right he proved to be. His successor, Field-Marshal von Kluge, and Rommel would both be dead in a few weeks' time. Both killed by their own hand.

*

Epsom – victory or defeat? Montgomery had long been saying that he wanted Caen. When Epsom failed to give it to him, the critics concluded that it had been a costly defeat. We now know that Epsom picked up an infinitely greater prize than Caen. It destroyed the German potential for counter-attack. 'I wanted to wait another two days,' said General of the Waffen SS Paul Hausser, 'but Hitler insisted that the counter-attack be launched on the 29th June.'[25] 9th SS and 10th SS were hurried into battle before they were ready; 12th SS waited for orders that did not come; and only parts of the 1st SS and 2nd SS panzer divisions were present. The Epsom crisis forced the German command to turn away from its preparations to win back the initiative. It was forced into a different battle, and one it was not ready for. The 9th SS Hohenstaufen and 10th SS Frundsberg Divisions were swallowed up in the defence of Hill 112. There they remained throughout July,

* Army Group 'B' order Ia Nr 4255/44.

This monument to the men the 15th Scottish Division situated on the side of the roa leading south to th Tourmauville bridge.

The Tourmauville bridg remains just as it was fort years ago. The Odon hardl deserves the name river.

being moved only after the Americans had achieved their breakout at Avranches.

Montgomery never under-estimated the toughness of the German soldier and the drive, initiative and experience of the German commanders. Ultra had told him of the SS panzer divisions arriving in Normandy. It was part of his bigger plan to keep them away from the Americans, who were battling for a suitable start-line for their breakout attack in the west. Once he realised that Epsom was pulling in the newly arrived German armour, he took no chances. The British would have a tough job holding them. The risk was great: a major defeat. He closed down Epsom and went into defence.

The original objective, Caen, had faded into the background. Of interest, however, is just how close Epsom came to gaining it. Rommel had already agreed to a withdrawal from the city, and he informed the German Seventh Army at midnight on the 30th June. Hitler intervened and cancelled it.[26]

A turning point had been reached in the Normandy campaign. It was not a deliberate result of Montgomery's Epsom plan. His repute as a general, however, rests firmly on his quick appreciation of the situation as it developed in favour of the bigger picture, and his readiness to close Epsom down at the point where it had yielded the maximum advantage. He had saved 11th Armoured Division from further confrontation and losses on Hill 112. It was able to join 7th Armoured and the Guards Armoured Division, giving Montgomery a flexibility that would allow him to strike hard again. He would be able to keep the German command dancing to his tune.

Nobody on the Allied side realised the significance of the Epsom battle at the time, and it is ironic that the following weeks brought increasing criticism of Montgomery in high places, and serious efforts were made to remove him from his command. Von Rundstedt and Rommel, and some of the shrewder German generals in Normandy, were aware, however, that they had already lost the battle.

Battlegroup Weidinger
2 SS Pz DIV

CHAPTER ELEVEN

Death Valley

'It stands for cruel battle, for courage and for bravery; it stands also for human frailty, for fear and for cowardice.'[6]

Yet there is nothing spectacular about Hill 112. It rises gently from the valley of the Odon river, which is itself little more than a stream. The tourist in his fast car travelling west out of Caen along the Route Nationale Nr 175 would find it difficult to believe that he is driving through what was known as 'Death Valley'. It was the stretch of road that saw the heaviest bombardment of the Normandy campaign. And that rounded dome of green countryside south of the road! Is that Hill 112? It scarcely warrants a glance. But in 1944 British and German soldiers crouched there through the long hot summer days and short nights with fear in their souls as they hung on grimly to their little bit of ground. The survivors would agree with the historian of the British 11th Armoured Division, who wrote that 'all the fighting was cruel and memory of the place is bitter'.

The little wood that stands on the top cannot be seen from this side. It was not really a wood at all. In 1944 it was an orchard surrounded by a hedge from which small trees were growing. Through the middle ran a ditch, from one side to the other, cutting the orchard in two; tall trees lined the ditch. After five weeks of bombardment all that remained was a clump of spike-like bare branches stretching in supplication towards the heavens. One German soldier likened it to a crown of thorns.

In the Epsom battles the Shermans of 11th Armoured Division had fought there with the panzers of the Hitler Youth, and the soldiers of the Rifle Brigade had occupied the wood for a short time before they were withdrawn on 29th June. It then fell into the hands of the 10th SS Frundsberg Panzer Division, and they were still there on this first week in July. They remember the wood as '*das Wäldchen der halben*

1944: '. . . a crown of thorns.'

1984: 'Croix des Filandriers' The 'little wood' can be seen in the background.

The Colleville – Cheux road.

He's looking for that tell-tale cloud of dust. This German artillery observer is using the cover of an overturned Sherman (Firefly) of 11th Armoured Division.

Bäume', literally 'the little wood of half-trees'. The panzer crews of the 102 SS Tiger Battalion called it '*das Kästenwäldchen*', the 'little box-shaped wood'. Many men of the Duke of Cornwall's Light Infantry were killed there, and they would refer to it as 'Cornwall Wood'. Welshmen of the 53rd Division named it quite simply 'Diamond Wood', for that was the shape of the patch of green it made on their maps.

Nearby, on the road that runs over the top of the hill, there still stands a wayside calvary, the Croix des Filandriers. Shells and bombs fell all round it during five weeks of bombardment. It is made of concrete, and it never received a direct hit. The German soldiers saw it silhouetted against the sky from the other side of the plateau, standing indestructible amidst the exploding shells and drifting smoke. It made a powerful impression, which is why they called 112 Calvary Hill.

*

Panzer Group West* had started life as the powerful armoured force that was to defeat any invasion attempt. It had early in the Normandy struggle been tied down in defence under command of the German Seventh Army. At the end of the Epsom battles it had been made independent, an army in its own right. It was holding the front against the British and Canadians. The German Seventh Army faced the Americans. The two German formations were part of Army Group 'B', under command of Field-Marshal Rommel. The command of Panzer Group West had been taken over by Panzer General Eberbach, a specialist tank leader with much experience of battle against the Russians. Of the eight panzer divisions fighting in Normandy, seven were in Panzer Group West and one was with the German Seventh Army. It was now the task of Montgomery to prevent those seven panzer divisions on the British front from being transferred from the Caen area to prevent an American breakout.

At midnight on 3rd/4th July the Germans started to bombard the Odon valley with heavy concentrations of shells and mortar bombs. The war diary of Panzer Group West states that 1,826 guns and mortars were to be used.

Missiles crashed down into villages now abandoned by the French civilians. Tiles clattered down from gaping roofs. Doors and windows hung at uncertain angles from broken walls. Tattered curtains fluttered in clouds of dust. Smoke drifted about. There was always something

* Later renamed the Fifth Panzer Army.

Graves of men of the Royal Engineers killed by shell and mortar fire whilst repairing the road at Colleville.

'Dead cows . . . match-stick legs pointing skywards . . .'

on fire, and always a smell of burning rubber. But overpowering all else and ever present was the smell of death. It got into the hair, into the uniform, it wouldn't go away. Dead cows, blown up, skin-stretched carcasses, matchstick legs pointing skywards, littered the fields. Blackened, burnt-out vehicles, lorries, halftracks, tanks, stood reared up on embankments, stuck nose-down in ditches, some on their sides, some even upside-down. Telephone wires cascaded from splintered poles to lie in tangles on the roadway.

For the first ten days of July the Germans were sitting firmly on top of the hill and the British were down in the valley below. Every movement, right back to Cheux and beyond, brought showers of shells and Moaning Minnies. Colleville was a black spot. The engineers lost many men whilst working on the road there. The Welsh lost one hundred and fifty men in their first forty-eight hours in le Valtru. The 4th Wiltshires moved into Baron for two days and it cost them seventy casualties.

Many a soldier who inhabited this valley of death owed his life to the soft soil of the low ground. Shells and mortar bombs penetrated deeply, stifling the shrapnel and throwing great fountains of earth and stones in to the air. The Monmouths buried fifty-three men in this area. The 2nd Battalion learned about living in a slit trench at Mondrainville:

> It became our home and had a fair chance of becoming one's last habitation on the face of the abused earth. Almost every day some domestic improvement was carried out; a little scraped out here to fit a 'knees-up' sleep position, a piece of head-cover against flying metal, a recess pried out for a cigarette tin or Sten gun magazine. I would lean on the edge of it at stand-to, looking out towards the sunset horizon and the coming stars, like any suburbanite leaning on his gateway after an evening of improving his garden. But reveries were subject to cruel and explosive interruptions. One night my next-door neighbours had a shell come at a slant slap into their home in the ground. On such tragedies one felt nothing but blazing anger. A senior officer stood up against the starry sky and, over the moans of the wounded, shook his fist and threatened the enemy with all they eventually got. The next 'crump' made one hug the lowest extremity of the trench with a naked feeling at the base of the spine. Then there were the 'duds', which hit the ground with sickening thuds, and left an expectation where there should have been an explosion.[27]

Herbert Fuerbringer could have told that 'senior officer' that his threat was already being fulfilled. He was not far away, dug in with the 19th SS Panzer Grenadiers on the crossroads between Rauray and Grainville. As company runner he was spending much of his time dodging the British 'stonks':

> My nerves were always on edge. I tried not to think that the next bang might be curtains for me. Perhaps, after all, I was splinter proof as my friends kept telling me. But the dreadful sights I kept running into on the battlefield were having their effect. One morning as I sat crouched in the dugout under heavy shell fire I noticed one of the medical orderlies looking at my hands. They were trembling. 'Why don't you have a cigarette?' he said. 'It'll keep your mind off it!' My pack was full of cigarettes. I used to save them all up to send to my father. So I smoked one cigarette after the other. I must have got through at least thirty. I might as well die from cigarette smoking as any other way. I don't remember whether the cigarettes did my nerves any good, but I do remember the name on the packet; it was 'Memphis'.

*

At the start of Epsom, Montgomery had said that he would keep the British battling on the eastern flank. Epsom had finished and the Americans were still not ready to launch their breakout offensive in the west. Monty would have to keep the pressure on at Caen. In directive M505 dated 30th June he told his army commanders that on no account could they remain inactive. Without initiative they could not win.

The Canadians were sent in to clear the Hitler Youth Division out of the aerodrome at Carpiquet. They failed. The light of battle seemed to have faded from their eyes. The divisional commander had lasted just four weeks. He had become a battle-weary, dispirited man.

Montgomery had to think again. On 7th July the British I Corps was launched on a frontal attack on Caen itself. 'We desperately wanted the Germans to believe this attack on Caen was the main Allied effort,' said Bradley, the American army commander.

Four hundred and sixty Halifax and Lancaster heavy bombers dropped two thousand six hundred tons of bombs: not on the German defences at the northern approaches to the city, for the degree of accuracy was not sufficient to ensure the safety of the British and

Men of the Wessex Division holding the forward trenches near Baron.

Canadian soldiers forming up to attack, but on the city itself to knock out the German supply lines. Caen, already greatly destroyed by the air raids of the first days of the liberation, entered its final martyrdom. Many French citizens who had survived earlier bombardments were killed. Two days later, the heaps of rubble that had once been Caen north of the river Orne were in British and Canadian hands; but the suburbs south of the river remained under German control.

The need to keep the pot boiling on the British front had become increasingly urgent. The Americans had been attacking for a week and had made little progress. The 2nd SS Das Reich Division had turned up on their front, and soon they would find that the Panzer Lehr was there, too. Monty had been trying to prevent that.

The battle for Caen had died down on 9th July. That same night the British side of Hill 112 was alive with movement. Battles have a habit of starting at dawn. For the soldiers who fight them that means no sleep, a tiring night of movement followed by a battle in which nervous energy struggles to hold exhaustion at bay.

The 43rd Wessex Division had been spared the tough battles of Epsom. Now it was their turn. They were to capture Hill 112 and drive south around the eastern side of the hill, through Château Fontaine and Eterville, to the village of Maltot and the river Orne beyond. In support would be the 31st and 4th Tank Brigades.

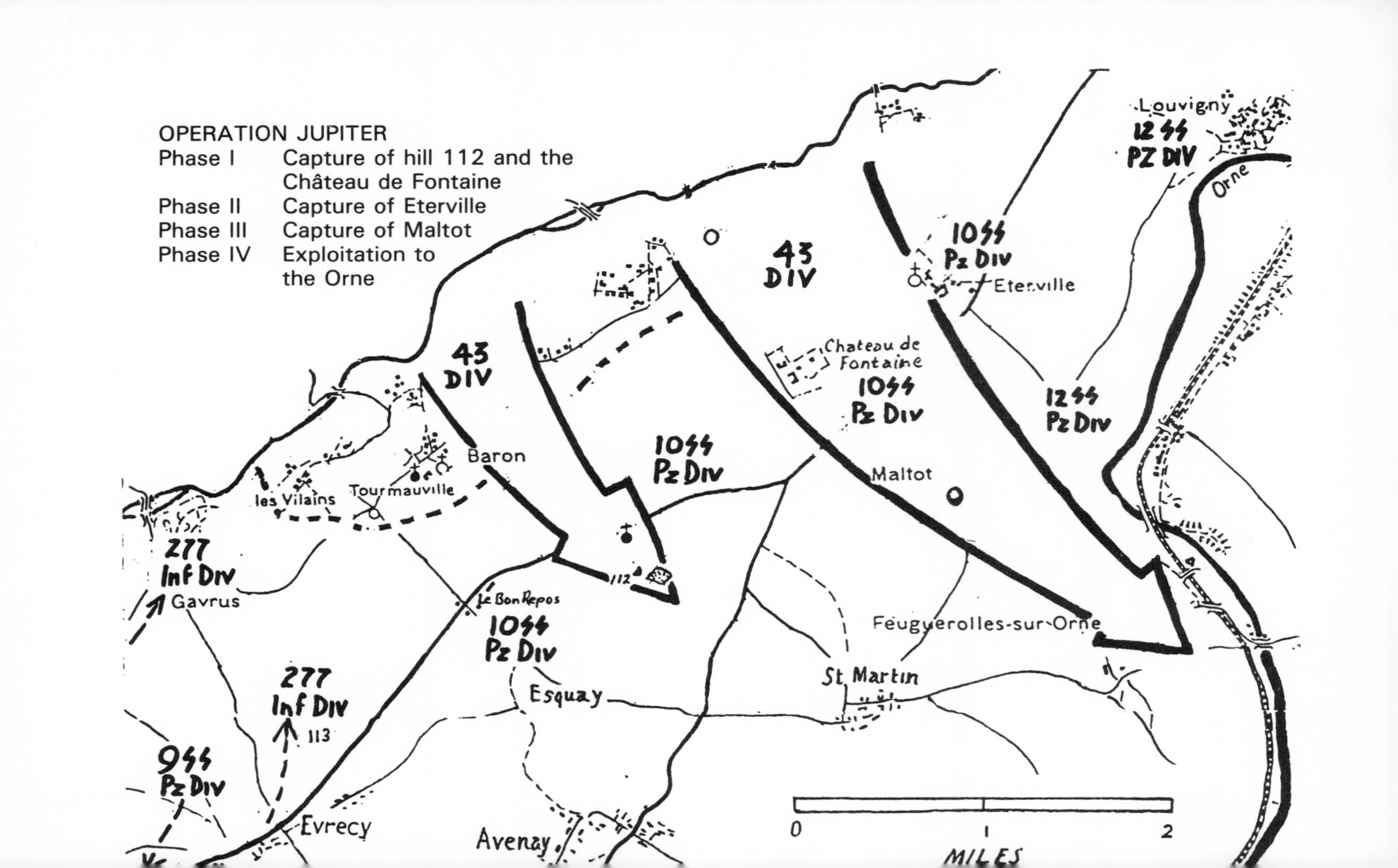

OPERATION JUPITER
Phase I Capture of hill 112 and the Château de Fontaine
Phase II Capture of Eterville
Phase III Capture of Maltot
Phase IV Exploitation to the Orne
Louvigny
12 SS PZ DIV
Orne
10 SS Pz Div
Eterville
43 DIV
Chateau de Fontaine
10 SS Pz Div
12 SS Pz Div
43 DIV
Baron
10 SS Pz Div
Maltot
les Vilains
Tourmauville
277 Inf Div
Gavrus
112
le Bon Repos
10 SS Pz Div
Feuguerolles-sur-Orne
St Martin
Esquay
277 Inf Div
113
9 SS Pz Div
Evrecy
Avenay
0
1
2
MILES

Hill 112 is a ten-acre plateau that slopes away on three sides. Except for a few hedges and the little wood there is no cover. There was much standing corn, and the red poppies brought thoughts of Flanders fields and that earlier war.

A lot of muck was going to be flying about. The massed guns of four British divisions* and two Army Groups Royal Artillery would see to that. So would the enemy, who, in addition to the divisional artillery, had two brigades of Moaning Minnies in support.

The 10th SS Frundsberg Division was sitting on top of the hill, the Hitler Youth was holding the Caen side, and on the western flank the 9th SS Hohenstaufen Division was that night completing a handover to the 277th Infantry Division (Wehrmacht).

A nasty surprise was avaiting the men of Wessex. At a quarter to three in the morning a battalion of new Tiger tanks arrived on the German side of the hill and moved into the village of St Martin. These fifty-six ton Tigers were Germany's most feared weapon. Neither the British nor the Americans had anything to compare with them. There were never more than three battalions of them fighting in Normandy, and all fought on the British sector. The 102 SS Heavy Tank Battalion was the Tiger battalion of the 11 SS Panzer Corps. It had been eighteen days on the road from Holland. It should have been in the 11 SS Panzer Corps counter-attack on the Scottish Corridor. It was just as well for the British that they had failed to turn up, for had these 'Kings of the Battlefield' been present at Cheux and le Valtru, who knows what the outcome might have been.

As dawn streaked the sky in the east the British bombardment suddenly flashed brighter in the sky above Hill 112. The distant sound of the guns was followed by a scream and howl as shells crashed down amongst the Tiger tanks in the orchards of St Martin :

> Günther Hensel, who was standing on the back of a tank, fell full length into a bed of flowers. A piece of shrapnel had taken off the back of his head. Poor Günther, who had looked forward with such impatience to his first battle. Now he was dead. Paul came forward to take his place.[28]†

The attack of the Wessex Division on Hill 112 had started.

* 43rd Wessex, 15th Scottish, 53rd Welsh and the artillery of 11th Armoured Division, which was still in the area.

† Will Fey, 102 SS Heavy Panzer Battalion.

43 WESSEX DIV

CHAPTER TWELVE

Lance-Corporal Butt blows the bugle

Captain Perks was found 'gazing over the field of battle quoting' Shakespeare:

> And gentlemen in England now abed
> Shall think themselves accurs't they were not here;
> And hold their manhood cheap whiles any speaks
> That fought with us upon Hill 112.

The battle had started at dawn. It was beginning to get light, and 'the whole scene was illuminated by burning carriers and tanks. Flame-throwers were in action. The enemy, using Nebelwerfers, was mortaring the advancing troops. Practically every weapon was in use – rifles, grenades, phosphorus, machine-guns and tanks – and casualties were extremely heavy.'[29*]

The riflemen were climbing the slope of Hill 112. It would be a different battalion that came down three days later. In that time four hundred casualties would have passed through the hands of the regimental aid post.

At the top of the hill the Somersets would find the Voie Romaine, a dead straight track dating back to the legions of Julius Caesar. It must have been used, also, by William the Conqueror, for it carries his name: Chemin du Duc Guillaume. At the top, where it crosses the lateral road between Eterville in the east and Evrecy in the west, stands a stone calvary, the Croix des Filandriers. The Chemin du Duc Guillaume, a rough track, continues south across the plateau summit to the little box-shaped wood and then runs on down the southern slope to St Martin.

*

* Sergeant Hole, 4th Battalion Somerset Light Infantry.

> A wounded man came running past; others were lying dead or wounded on the ground; but the motor of the towing carrier was still running; not wanting to leave behind a perfectly good anti-tank gun, I decided to drive the carrier myself.

Captain Perks was the commander of the anti-tank guns of the 4th Somerset Light Infantry. The British artillery barrage was dropping short, and a shell had exploded causing casualties amongst the waiting gun crews. It was five o'clock in the morning when the battalion emerged from the trees of Baron village and started the ascent up the slope of Hill 112. It was one thousand five hundred yards of open country. The battalion would be under enemy observation all the way. Enemy shells and mortar bombs were falling. Captain Perks kept just to the rear of the commanding officer:

> About half-way up the CO's driver was hit. Shrapnel had gone right through his skull from one side to the other. I helped to get him out.

Those little puffs of smoke in the sky looked harmless enough, but they were sending down showers of splinters. For Major Wardle they brought to an end the five minutes of battle for which he had been training for five years: 'I didn't feel anything. But with all the other men I was lying on the ground.'[8]

The battalion was using the track of Duc Guillaume as a centre line. Three German helmets bobbed up in the tall corn. A panzerfaust was fired at one of the supporting Churchill tanks; it burst into flames. The commanding officer of the Somersets threw a grenade, but it was the intelligence officer, Captain Bennetts, who seized a Bren gun and killed those who had fired.

Just below the summit, on the Eterville road, there were hedgerows and German dugouts and trenches. A close combat infantry battle developed. Captain Perks was in the middle of it:

> I was throwing grenades into dugouts where the Germans were hidden. Then I was wounded in the side. A shell splinter, I think. A violent tank battle developed on the northern slopes. I had guns, but by this time there were not enough men to man them. The corn was so high that we couldn't use the gun sights. We aimed by guess-work. Soon three German tanks were in flames and a fourth was beating a hasty retreat with smoke pouring out of the turret.

THE 43rd WESSEX DIVISION ATTACK ON HILL 112
AND MALTOT
10th-11th July 1944

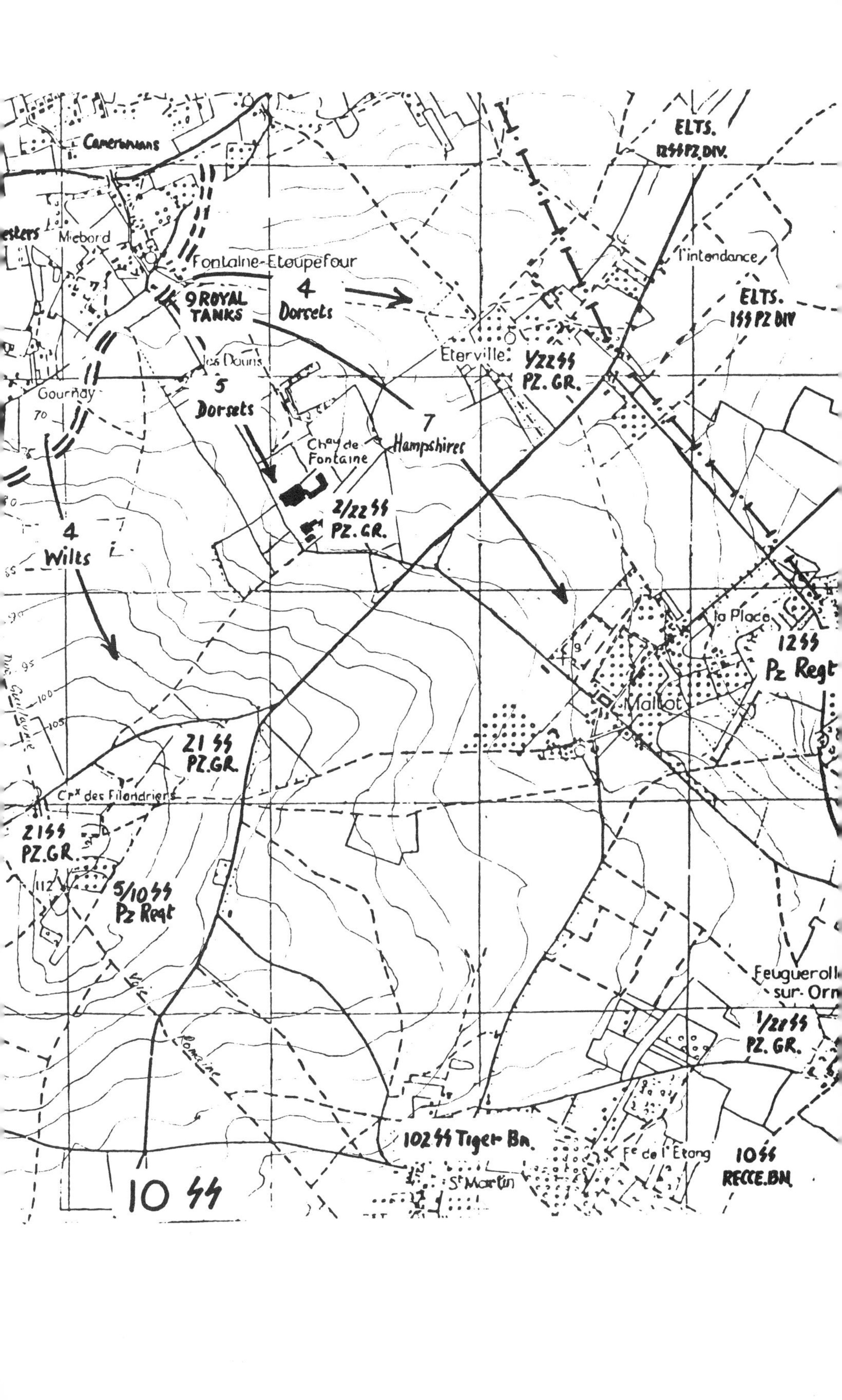
Cameronians
Miebord
Fontaine-Etoupefour
9 ROYAL TANKS
4 Dorsets
ELTS. 12 SS PZ. DIV.
l'intendance
ELTS. 1 SS PZ DIV
Eterville
1/22 SS PZ. GR.
les Douets
5 Dorsets
Gournay
7 Hampshires
Ch^au de Fontaine
2/22 SS PZ. GR.
4 Wilts
la Place
12 SS Pz Regt
Maltot
21 SS PZ. GR.
Cr^x des Filandriers
21 SS PZ. GR.
112
5/10 SS Pz Regt
Feugueroll sur-Orn
1/22 SS PZ. GR.
Voie Romaine
102 SS Tiger Bn.
F^e de l'Etang
10 SS RECCE. BN.
St Martin
10 SS

By nine o'clock the Somersets had reached the line of the Eterville road. The German forward positions, about a company strong, had been overrun. The dead lay in the trenches and clustered around two anti-tank guns. Three Mark IV panzers had been on the hilltop in support. They had been destroyed, but not before giving warning to others. A second troop had hurried up the hill to help in the defence; the leader had been knocked out, the crew killed; the others had reversed back behind the crest. But the price paid by the Somersets had been heavy. Their dead and wounded lay in the corn; three of the four rifle company commanders were amongst the casualties; one company had lost all its officers. They had reached the road. The solid stone cross of the calvary stood there, defiant in the shell fire. Beyond was the plateau, a large area about a mile square. The next task of the Somersets was to clear it.

The German defence had by now been fully alerted. This was a full scale British attack. The 10th SS Frundsberg Panzer Regiment had sent three of its companies racing along the road to Esquay. There they ran full tilt into the infantrymen of the Wiltshire Regiment, who had climbed the slope of the hill on the right of the Somersets. There had been less opposition here, and they had pushed one company over the crest. It was now caught exposed on the open hillside. The le Bon Repos crossroads lay just ahead of them, and beyond was Esquay. The Germans opened up. One panzer rolled up the road spraying the prostrate men on either side with its machine-guns until it was knocked out with a PIAT. But this forward British company was nailed to the ground, it was losing men, and it could get neither forward nor back.

The top of Hill 112 had almost disappeared in the fumes, smoke and dust of battle. The 10th SS Frundsberg artillery, the multiple mortars of the 8th Werfer Brigade and the 88 mm guns of the flak batteries were pounding the plateau with high explosive. In the sky above were the ever-present 'Jabos' of the Allied airforces, circling and diving through the tracer of the lighter German flak guns.

Screen off the enemy mortars and artillery across the river Orne! That was the task of Major Duke, observation officer of the Royal Artillery with the infantry advancing on the other side of the Somersets.* This battalion had done what the Scotsmen did at Epsom: the two forward assault companies had overrun the German infantry before they emerged from their deep shelters. They had gained the crest with little difficulty. A mile away on the lower ground in front of them lay the village of Maltot. Running across the fields in that direction were retreating German infantrymen. Meanwhile, on the slope behind, the

* On the right of the Somersets were the 5th Wilts, on the left the 4th Wilts.

German positions they had by-passed had come to life and were offering resistance to the British troops following up.

It was through this confused battle, avoiding the bodies of the killed and wounded in the corn, that Major Duke now took his halftrack. From the higher ground he could see, two and a half miles away, the line of the Orne river. It didn't take him long to hide it in thick grey smoke. He had finished and was about to move when the gunner in front of the halftrack opened fire. On the right, on the higher ground of Hill 112, were German infantry. Then came into view the long menacing barrels of three Tiger tanks. A solid 88 mm shot slammed into the halftrack. Major Duke's left arm was completely shattered; his right hand was a mass of blood.*

The Tiger tanks that had early that morning arrived in St Martin had joined the battle. Two companies, about twenty panzers in number, had first moved up the German slope and halted at the hedge facing the little wood from the east. They were above the morning mist; the sun was trying to break through. Allied aeroplanes suddenly swooped out of the sky, dropped their bombs, circled and dived with all machine-guns firing. It was the 10th SS Panzer Grenadiers who suffered the casualties. The noise deadened the senses. The hilltop was being pounded by shellfire. Nothing of the fierce battle raging there could be seen.

Commanding the 2nd Company was Hauptsturmfuehrer (Captain) Endemann. His wireless wasn't working. He was transmitting orders by hand signal. He took the company past the little box-shaped wood and on to the plateau. Corporal Piller's Tiger was immediately hit and had to pull back. Rathsack fired and knocked out a British tank. Untersturmfuehrer (Lieutenant) Schroif knocked out two more and an anti-tank gun. Endemann disappeared into the smoke and dust and was not seen or heard of again.

The 3rd Company moved on to the eastern side of the plateau. Hans Richter was a Tiger commander with this company:

> A solid armour-piercing shot went clean through the turret. It took with it the head of the gunner, Hans Kruckner. It took also my left forearm and smashed my right one. It peppered my chest with bits of metal and sent a splinter into my right eye. That was the end for us. I was sure that I would bleed to death. 'Reverse!' I shouted. The

* Major Duke lost his left arm, a finger from his right hand and some of his hearing.

> gun-loader tore at my headphones. He tied the cable around my left upper arm to stop the bleeding. I was getting weaker. But I managed to get out of the turret. This is it, I thought, as I staggered across an open field in a din of crashing shellfire. Another Tiger came roaring past. It stopped. 'We'll take you!' Strong arms lifted me up. First on to the back of the panzer, and then, when the firing got worse, into the turret. I lay semi-conscious on the turntable. I remember an ambulance – doors open – the entrance to a village. I heard someone say: 'Main artery! Take him! Quickly!'[16*]

Little wonder that for the Churchills of the 7th Royal Tank Regiment, which were supporting the Somersets, things got steadily worse:

> . . . Lieutenant Colonel Gaisford blinded in one eye and Major Fleming killed in his tank. 'C' Squadron suffered terribly, losing six tanks... The Somersets were decimated.[12†]

The Somersets would be lucky to hold on to what they had won. Of the sixteen rifle company officers who had moved up the hill, only four remained. One company was under the command of a sergeant. The carrier platoon commander, who was to have arrived with his men to help clear the plateau, was dead. The surviving Churchill tanks had pulled back to hull-down positions. And it was there, on the reverse slope hidden by the crest, that the Somersets were digging in. They had left only lightly manned observation posts higher up along the line of the road.

The seizing of Hill 112 was only part of the British plan. The enemy had to be driven from there because only then could the 43rd Wessex Division send infantry and tanks south across the lower, eastern slopes of the hill, through Château de Fontaine, Eterville and Maltot, and finally to the bridges over the Orne. That was the task of the Dorsets and Hampshires. During the night they had marched forward and concentrated in Verson and Fontaine Etoupefour.

*

Hauptsturmfuehrer (Lieutenant) Willi Kaendler, commander of a troop of tanks with the Hitler Youth Division, was worried by that smoke that Major Duke had put down along the line of the river. He

* Richter – in a letter to *Der Freiwillige* – Jan. '76.
† Major Joscelyne, 7th RTR.

had been on the road running along the river bank since dawn. The panzers of No 5 Company were spread out widely in defence, for the road was the only supply route for the elements of the Hitler Youth Division still hanging on to the suburbs of Caen this side of the Orne. With them were also some panzer grenadiers of the 1st SS Adolf Hitler Division, and hidden in the woods along the river bank near Maltot, away from the eyes of the Allied airforces, was the surviving armour of the 12th SS Panzer Regiment, some thirty panzers, ten of them Panthers. They had been pulled out of Caen the day before.

Kaendler decided to push forward into the smoke. He came to the trenches of some panzer grenadiers. They were nervous. What was happening? Nobody knew. He pushed on and emerged from the smoke to see a British Bren carrier racing along the Fontaine Etoupefour road. He fired. It went up in flames. The British were attacking the Château de Fontaine. Through the smoke and haze of battle further west, Kaendler could see British tanks and infantry on the slope of Hill 112. This was a full-scale British offensive. He sent back over the air a warning to the 12th SS Hitler Youth Panzer Regiment. But he had moved across the divisional boundary and was in the 10th SS Frundsberg sector. His company commander warned him over the air not to get involved in the battle. He returned to his defensive position on the river bank not far from Eterville, but not before opening fire and claiming several Churchill tanks as victims.

At a quarter-past-six the 5th Dorsets signalled that Château de Fontaine was in its hands. It was an optimistic claim. Fierce battle had brought confusion. The château had been the headquarters of the 2nd Battalion of the 22nd Frundsberg Panzer Grenadier Regiment. These Waffen SS soldiers were still contesting every yard.

The report of success at the château was the signal for the 4th Dorsets to advance with Churchill and flame-throwing tanks on the village of Eterville:

> Lance-Corporal Butt sounded the charge on his bugle. The battalion rose to its feet as one man, many cheered. It was a wonderful experience – we were all glad at that moment to be there.[30*]

German infantry dug in on the first rise were quickly overrun. The Dorsets pushed on rapidly, leaving dead and wounded in the cornfields behind them. Enemy shellfire was falling; carriers and trucks were burning. They reached the approaches to Eterville close behind the

* Major Symonds, 4th Dorsets.

moving barrage. Aircraft roared past overhead. The men looked up – three white bands on the fuselage – 'Ours!' Then they saw the bombs, little black specks falling towards them. Two fell in their midst, throwing up stones and earth in great clouds of dust. There were casualties, but only one man was killed. Over the village hung oily black clouds of billowing smoke. The flame-throwing Crocodiles (Churchill tanks) were burning out the opposition.

Hauptsturmfuehrer (Captain) Richter, commander of the 1st Battalion SS Frundsberg Panzer Grenadiers, had spent that night visiting the forward companies in defence of Eterville. At dawn he and his company runner were on their way back to battalion headquarters when a torrent of British shell fire suddenly descended:

> It took us more than an hour to cover seven hundred yards. We arrived just as a messenger came in from our reserve position: 'Enemy tanks level with us across the boundary with 1st SS!' Off went Sturmmann Schwingler and the company runners with my orders: 'Pull back into Eterville immediately!' The artillery barrage was now deafening and smoke was being mixed with the high-explosive. Grenadiers arrived from Château de Fontaine carrying the seriously wounded commander of the 2nd Battalion. 'Richter! – Richter!' he kept saying to me, 'Save my battalion! – Save my battalion!' More and more wounded started to come in from the 1st Battalion positions, and then panzer grenadiers who had managed to get away when the Château de Fontaine defences were overrun.[37]

It was nine o'clock when Sturmmann Schwingel burst into the headquarters in Eterville. He was out of breath, had one jackboot on and the other in his hand. 'Forward companies taken prisoner!' he gasped. '*Engländer* two hundred yards away with small tracked vehicles and infantry!'

The shells were now whining and whistling past overhead. The bombardment was falling further back in the area of Maltot. The smoke, too, was drifting away. Shells from British tanks were, however, soon crashing into the western wall of the German headquarters building; the upper storeys were collapsing in showers of dust, stone and plaster. Solid shot broke through into the partly-raised cellar that housed the headquarters staff. The entrance hall was a confusion of wounded men being helped or being carried to the safer side of the building. Beneath the trees outside a large German signals' truck was burning. Time was short. The battalion commander gave the order to move out. But what of the wounded? The commander turned to the medical officer, Dr Moeferdt: 'We can't leave them on their own! You'll have to stay!'

The words hardly registered with the hard-pressed medical officer. He had only two medical orderlies to help him; he was surrounded by the wounded and the dying. And so it came as a shock when a little later figures with blackened faces, holding guns at the ready, finger on the trigger, rushed in and started to shout at him:

> I couldn't understand what they were saying, but it was clear we were meant to put our hands up. All who could manage to walk were ordered out – not many other than the orderlies. My efforts to make them understand that I was a doctor, that I should be allowed to stay and look after the wounded, were to no avail.[37]

It was the padre of the 4th Dorsets who intervened and released the German medical officer and the two orderlies. Oblivious of the falling shells they worked on in co-operation with the British medical staff:

'I have a vivid recollection of the efficiency of the German medical personnel whom we captured, who worked hard at bringing in our wounded as well as their own...'[30*]

The leading assault groups had already passed through the village without great opposition when the battle flared up behind them.

Hauptsturmfuehrer Richter and the German headquarters staff were rallying groups of survivors in Eterville and from the Château de Fontaine. They were fighting back in the gardens and along the tall thick hedges of dense foliage. Machine-gun bullets were tearing across farmhouse walls in spurts of dust and splinters of stonework. Then down came the showers of German shells and mortar bombs that were always thrown at villages they had just lost.

> Everyone dug like hell... All we had with us was an entrenching tool, which proved useless; to speed up the digging several of us sifted the earth out with our bare hands...[30†]

A thousand yards away in the west rows of khaki-clad figures were advancing through the corn towards Maltot. The attack of the Hampshires had just started.

They were seen by the German battalion commander. It was time for him to move back with the remnants of the two battalions of panzer

* Sergeant Caines, 4th Dorsets.
† Sergeant Caines.

grenadiers. They pulled back across the fields, moving also in the direction of the river and Maltot.

The sight of the dead on the battlefield was new to the men of the Dorsets. This was their first battle:

> I saw beneath some long grass a dead Jerry. At first he looked alive, his face seemed to have plenty of colour and his body showed no markings of death. I was really afraid to touch him, for we had all been well drilled as to the possibility of dead bodies being booby-traps. Grenades were stuck in his belt, his rifle in his hand and his helmet was still on his head, he had washed and shaved. I bucked up my courage and touched him to make sure he was a dead one. Yes, he was all right, but whether he was booby-trapped or not, I didn't bother to find out.[30*]

Back at the bridge over the Odon there was the traffic jam that accompanied every major British attack. A reserve battalion was urgently wanted at Château Fontaine. Military police had pushed all vehicles off the road. The bridge was an enemy target. Bringing up the rear of the infantry column was Captain Marshall, the medical officer:

> A salvo of shells dropped. . . We found a despatch rider on the road – killed outright. . . Two engineer officers had been thrown into the river . . .[31†]

An ambulance had been hit, wounding those inside a second time. No one could find the driver.

Movement in the area of Château Fontaine was still dangerous. 'That's the fifth pot-shot that bastard's taken at me!' The 'bastard' was found submerged in the duck pond. Another sniper – 'he couldn't have been more than seventeen years old' – was found buried in the mud of a ditch, covered with slime and weeds. Another was hidden in a hayrick and only discovered when it caught fire. Others fought to the death in barns and outhouses. Enemy trenches were full of the dead. The carcasses of farm animals lay everywhere: the air was putrid and thick with flies.

About eighty prisoners had been taken. A platoon of the Dorsets, about thirty men under Lieutenant Hayes, had disappeared in the confusion of battle: it would be several days before a night patrol would stumble over their dead bodies.

* Sergeant Caines, 4th Dorsets.
† Captain Marshall, attached 7th Somersets.

Next over the Odon bridge were Scottish troops* on their way to take over from the 4th Dorsets in Eterville. They came under shell-fire and were suffering casualties all along the route. The commanding officer, who had gone on ahead, found the sunken road blocked with carriers. The dead and wounded lay everywhere, amongst them an army photographer, killed, his camera broken.† Repeated requests for ambulances and stretcher-bearers had to be refused : back in Fontaine Etoupefour the medical services were already fully stretched.

At the far end of Eterville Major Symonds had just sited his company in defence when he saw across the fields in the direction of the river enemy panzers and infantry :

> I began to dig my own slit trench. I had only got the top soil removed when one of the hundreds of shells and bombs that were showered on us tipped me into my own works. I was unconscious through loss of blood for a little. When I came round, my Canadian second-in-command, Captain Ron With, had stopped the bleeding for me. I was able to hand over the message to go to battalion headquarters for orders to attack Maltot. . . The 7th Hampshires had failed to capture it.[30]

The Hampshires were in trouble. That morning they had pushed south through the cornfields between Château de Fontaine and Eterville and ascended the ridge to cross the lateral road. On the lower ground beyond they could see their objective, the village of Maltot. As they moved down the slope they drew the fire of the Hitler Youth Panzer Regiment hiding in the woods on the river bank east of the village. The Churchill tanks in support, hopelessly outgunned by an enemy they couldn't see, never reached Maltot. Twelve were destroyed, marked by plumes of black smoke rising from the corn : only two survivors scuttled back to the safety of hull-down positions behind the ridge.

Maltot, however, was not a strongpoint like Eterville and Château de Fontaine, and the Hampshires in the centre and on the right got into the village without heavy loss. Those on the left walked into the fire of the Hitler Youth panzers in the woods near the river bank and only about twenty men reached the road in Maltot.

A casualty on this eastern flank was the battalion headquarters wireless truck. Hit by a mortar bomb, it was then smashed by an anti-tank

* 9th Cameronians (15th Scottish Division).

† This explains the absence of photographs in the archives of the Imperial War Museum.

shell. The adjutant was wounded, the signals officer was missing and the medical officer was killed whilst attending to the casualties. The wireless link with brigade headquarters had gone.

Plotting the progress of the British offensive in his battle headquarters was the commander of the 10th SS Frundsberg Division, SS Oberfuehrer (Brigadier) Harmel:

> Whilst our divisional and the corps artillery, together with the mortars of the 8th Werfer Brigade, brought down a heavy curtain of fire to prevent the British from developing their attack on the top of Hill 112, the armoured battalion of the 21st SS Panzer Grenadier Regiment and the 10th SS Reconnaissance Battalion were moved forward to counter-attack at Maltot with the support of Tiger tanks from the 102 SS Heavy Battalion.[37]

Meanwhile the Hampshires had fought their way through Maltot and were digging in four hundred yards further south. The company on the left flank of the advance was missing. Then comes an entry in the battalion war diary: '0955 hours. . . Imperative to withdraw – Tiger tanks and infantry attacking from the south-east and the south-west.'

With the Tigers racing across from St Martin was Unterscharfuehrer (Corporal) Will Fey:

> Our four panzers led the reconnaissance into Maltot. We had to protect the flank of our Tiger tanks on Hill 112. Off we went at top speed over the open fields. We reached the edge of the village. Wasting no time, we pushed through the hedges. There, in front of us, were four Sherman tanks.* Two shots finished off the one on the left, the one next to him suffered the same fate, and the troop commander pushed forward to knock out a third. The fourth sought safety in racing back along the road. It was a great boost for our young panzer crew.[28]

Infantry pushing forward from Château Fontaine to try to make contact with the Hampshires ran into three more of these Tigers in a little wood west of Maltot. Captain 'Crasher' White, 'in a soft cap and brandishing a cane', rushed forward with two anti-tank guns. He was not seen again. These men of the 5th Dorsets could do nothing about those impregnable monsters. They were forced to retire leaving many dead in the corn.

* Not Shermans – probably self-propelled anti-tank guns.

A Tiger tank of the 102 SS Heavy Battalion (II SS Panzer Corps). Unteroffizier Will Fey, the commander, is on the left.

British 17-pounder anti-tank gun, knocked-out and burning on the slopes of Hill 112.

At a quarter-past-ten the commanding officer of the Hampshires was wounded. The battalion had attempted to form a strong-point around the crossroads in the village. In vain: there was no field of fire. It was pulling back to the higher ground north of the village.

There were about three hundred men left. 'B' Company could not be found. It had last been seen moving towards the wood near the river. Patrols sent out to bring it back failed to return. Heavy mortar fire and the loss of towing carriers prevented the battalion from hauling back more than two of the precious anti-tank guns. '*1035 hours* – enemy infiltrating through the orchards and cornfields – battalion's new defensive position being heavily shelled and mortared.'

The commanding officer, wound patched up, went round to each defensive position, exhorting and encouraging his men. There was to be no further withdrawal. The Hampshires would stay where they were and fight it out.

There had long been no communication with brigade. Calls for help from the artillery had brought no response. The supporting tanks had been wiped out. The 'poor bloody infantry' were on their own. An enemy counter-attack, panzers and infantry, was coming in. There is this entry in the war diary:

> It was not until the enemy were actually entering the battalion positions that the call for fire was finally granted. A very accurate barrage was laid just forward of the fields... This undoubtedly saved the position.

But for how long? The commanding officer, Lieutenant-Colonel Ray, was wounded again, this time it was to prove fatal. Since the beginning of the battle there had been no medical officer, no properly manned regimental aid post, and no ambulance to evacuate the wounded. Men were dying for lack of trained medical attention.

*

In the war diary of Panzer Group West this entry was made:

> In the course of the morning the enemy succeeded in capturing Eterville and Maltot. But all assaults on the dominating feature, Hill 112, were repulsed.

The sudden appearance of British infantry so close behind the artillery barrage had surprised the defence and overwhelmed the 10th SS panzer grenadiers before they were ready; it was a repeat of the success at Epsom. And once again that rumour of 'a new kind of shell' was brought in as an explanation. 'Using a lot of smoke and a new kind of shell . . . the British had broken through on a wide front between Hill 112 and Eterville.'[6]

But luck did not run for the Hampshires. The 12th SS Hitler Youth Panzer Regiment, pushed out of Caen the day before, had harboured in the wood on the river bank near Maltot, and the 102 SS Heavy Tank Battalion of the II SS Panzer Corps had at last arrived on its long journey from Holland. It had moved into the village of St Martin, a mile south of Maltot.

At midday Field-Marshal Rommel arrived at the headquarters of Panzer Group West. What was happening at Hill 112? It was the dominating feature on which the whole Normandy battle was pivoted. Its fall would bring crisis and withdrawal along the whole front.

General Eberbach reassured him. A powerful counter-attack was being prepared and would go in before nightfall. At three o'clock that morning the 9th SS Hohenstaufen Division had finished its handover of the western side of the salient to the 277th Infantry Division. It had been on its way out when the British attack broke. It was now on its way back and would counter-attack through 10th SS both at Hill 112 and at Maltot and Eterville. Meanwhile the Tiger tank battalion of the Panzer Corps was being used to strengthen the defence.

*

It was three o'clock in the afternoon when the British commander, Major General Ivor Thomas, met his two brigade commanders to discuss the situation. Stalemate was staring them in the face – even worse at Maltot, where the desperate plight of the Hampshires was at last known. 'The hill must be taken no matter what the cost!' The brigadiers agreed with Major-General Thomas. Only if they could gain the dominating feature, Hill 112, would they be able to make progress at Maltot. They had just one battalion in reserve, the 5th Duke of Cornwall's Light Infantry. It was waiting at Fontaine Etoupefour. It would be brought across to attack at Hill 112. Meanwhile the Hampshires would have to be pulled out. They were given permission to withdraw.

*

Chester Wilmot, war correspondent with the BBC, was looking out over the cornfield towards the wood around Maltot:

> By now that wood was enveloped in smoke – not the black smoke of hostile mortars but white smoke laid by our guns as a screen for our infantry who were now being forced to withdraw.
>
> We could see them moving back through the waist-high corn, and out of the smoke behind them came angry flashes as the German tanks fired from Maltot. But even as the infantry were driven back another battalion was moving forward to relieve them, supported by Churchill tanks firing tracer over the heads of the advancing men. They moved right past our hedge and out across the corn. The Germans evidently saw them coming, for away off on our right flank machine-guns opened up and then the nebelwerfers . . .[35]

A straddle of Moaning Minnies sent Wilmot diving for cover, 'forcing as much of myself as possible into an old German dugout'. The Hampshires were withdrawing with three hundred of their men killed, wounded or missing. But someone had blundered. The Dorsets were already moving forward to help them. They found in Maltot not the Hampshires but the enemy Tiger and Panther tanks:

> Jerry must have been observing every move and allowed us to come right up close, thus cutting us off. Suddenly the whole party was cut down by a burst of fire from a Spandau. . . No one dared to put his head above the corn, as soon as Jerry observed the slightest movement a burst of fire would be the reply.[30*]

The high-velocity 88 mm cannon of the panzers opened up to the right of them and to the left of them. A blinding flash in the corn, and men were lying killed and wounded before the sound of the gun had reached them. A dull thud, a fountain of earth thrown into the air, and a Churchill tank was in flames. Carriers and anti-tank guns were being torn apart. The few Churchills not sending spirals of smoke into the air ran for the safety of the ridge behind them. What hope had they against the superior guns of the German tanks. Major Whittle kept going with his Bren carrier, 'with the corn almost level with the sides, and wishing it were much higher'.

For twenty-year old Corporal Portway a new horror suddenly arrived:

* Sergeant Caines, 4th Dorsets.

> A squadron of our own rocket-firing Typhoons dropped out of the sun in twos and threes with the noise of an express train: the field seemed to rise up in flames; there was a great noise of rending metal. Rooted to the spot, we gazed upwards as another plane dived; we saw the wings shudder as the rockets were released. Explosions tore at the tortured earth. We hung on with our bare hands clutching the soil. My comrade at my side had become a mass of gory rags. In front of me was the company despatch-rider, with no legs. A man came running out of the dust and smoke, total bewilderment on his face.[8]

The enemy action had split the battalion into isolated groups. The headquarters remained on the northern outskirts of the village, where it dug in and was joined by men who had lost contact. The rifle companies pushed on, harassed by enemy fire. Fighting amongst the gardens and houses they lost contact with each other and with battalion headquarters. Corporal Portway was with one of these groups, moving through the battered and burning village:

> Most of the flames gave off no smoke at all. We could feel the heat as we climbed over the debris. We came to a large hole in the ground. . . As usual, no one knew where we were going or what we were supposed to do. After the carnage in the fields no one felt particularly heroic. Utterly exhausted, we leaned against the wall. . . Suddenly above us was a German soldier. He was as surprised as we were; but in his raised hand was a stick grenade. We stopped feeling sorry for ourselves and made a dash for the furthest corner. . . A Sten gun rattled out; there was an explosion. . . The German lay in a pool of blood, half a magazine of bullets in his chest; he had fallen on to his own grenade.[8]

For three hours the Dorsets hung on. They were surrounded by enemy infantry and tanks concealed in the wooded areas, where they were difficult to locate. Control had been lost and Battalion headquarters had failed to regain contact with any of the rifle companies. It was almost nine o'clock in the evening when the commanding officer gave the order to withdraw. It failed to reach the men fighting in the village; all of 'A' Company and most of the other three rifle companies were left behind. Bringing up the rear of this sad withdrawal were Regimental Sergeant Major Drew and Sergeant Caines, who were helping a third man, a private soldier whose foot had been blown off:

These photographs of Maltot indicate the heavy fighting that took place there during the month of July 1944.

He had, till then, been hopping along on his rifle. He remained quite conscious and cheerful until we got him to a medical officer; only then did he pass out.[30]

Corporal Portway was one of the many men left behind:

. . . the rattle of the gunfire had gradually died away, leaving only a solitary rifle shot here and there. It was a strange silence, an eerie sense of solitude. There were five of us in a ditch. We knew what had happened. The battalion had gone. We hadn't heard the order. There was only one thing to do. Wait for darkness and then try to get back. . . Then the artillery opened up again. This time it was different; a scream of shells and the village became a hell on earth. We were at the wrong end of our own artillery bombardment. . . We pressed down deeply in the ditch, no longer completely in control of our actions, the fearful noise annihilating our senses. . . I kept my eye fixed on a dandelion close to my head. It was my anchor in this armageddon. Silence again; a silence as loud as was the noise. . . Then voices – German voices. Would they pass by? Then I saw blood trickling down on the shoulder of my jacket. The man next to me was dead. Gutteral voices and exclamations. Three German soldiers stood above us. We lifted our hands in the air.[8]

That morning when Lance-Corporal Butt sounded the charge on his bugle five hundred men had risen to their feet and cheered. They had stormed Eterville with a panache that had taken the SS defenders by surprise. Now, fourteen hours later, only five officers and less than eighty men had come back. Many lay dead with the Hampshires in Maltot, many were wounded. A few got back during the night; others were taken prisoner. The survivors were shattered and exhausted:

All of us were cold as stones, extremely worn out and dog tired. . . I myself felt fit to drop, it had been a terrible twenty-four hours, something I will never forget as long as I live, seeing men fall, and hearing the wounded cry and moan with pain as they were evacuated. I could never express in my own words the horror experienced that day.[30*]

* Sergeant Caines, 4th Dorsets.

CHAPTER THIRTEEN

The Crown of Thorns

Major Richard Joscelyne had every reason to feel worried:

> At 1700 hours I was sent for to report to Brigade headquarters. . . I listened with apprehension to their plan.[12]

With his squadron of fourteen Churchill tanks Major Joscelyne was to support the attack of the 5th Duke of Cornwall's Light Infantry on Hill 112. Like the Somersets, who were still there, dug in just below the crest, the DCLI were to use the Chemin du Duc Guillaume as a centre-line. An order to attack where others have failed to achieved the objective brings a feeling of dismay to even the doughtiest.

Much of the corn had been flattened. The slope was littered with the burnt-out hulks of tanks and other vehicles destroyed that morning; and there were the already rusting carcasses of Shermans of 11th Armoured Division knocked out in the earlier battles on Hill 112. There were slit trenches and shell craters everywhere, old and new. Abandoned items of military equipment gave witness to the fear and confusion of battles won and lost.

Lieutenant-Colonel James was twenty-six years old. Two weeks earlier he had been a major, a company commander with the Somersets. Now he was the commanding officer of the 5th Duke of Cornwall's Light Infantry. Promotion comes quickly in battle, particularly in the infantry. The former commanding officer had been killed at le Haut du Bosq on the battalion's first day of battle. So it was not surprising that Lieutenant-Colonel James should choose to set up his rear battalion headquarters in the positions of the 4th Somersets. He had been ordered to capture the little wood about five hundred yards away on the other side of the plateau. An artillery barrage with all available guns had been laid on.

Men of the Duke of Cornwall's Light Infantry digging in along a hedge near Verson. These were the men called forward to capture the top of Hill 112.

It was spitting with rain and the clouds were hastening the evening towards the dusk as the Cornishmen emerged from the woods near Baron on to the gently climbing slope of 112. It was a grim scene in a grey light. So the rumour was true then! The Somersets had caught a packet. Now it was the turn of the Cornishmen. The artillery barrage started.

In extended lines, with two companies forward, they moved over the crest. They saw the road and the wayside calvary. The plateau beyond was hidden in swirling smoke. Somewhere in the din and dust of the explosions was their objective. All went well until bursts of machine-gun fire swept across from the edge of the plateau on the left. Down went Major Vaudrey. He had been killed. The lead company suffered heavy casualties and failed to get forward. Others moved through. Some of the enemy had been killed, others, a few, had been taken prisoner: most ran back and disappeared below the far edge of the plateau. Of Major Vaudrey's Company only about forty men remained.

The advance on the right had gone more quickly. The enemy had retreated from the little wood, and Lieutenant Carmolli,* wound-up by the excitement of the battle, had dashed on down the German slope in pursuit; he was killed, as were most of those who followed him.

In the confusion of battle one company disappeared. It was thought to be somewhere further right, where a large enclosed paddock adjoined the little wood. The battalion, much reduced in strength, started to dig in along the two sides. The forward edge was left unoccupied. Lieutenant-Colonel James and his small combat headquarters occupied the ditch that ran through the centre. The battalion six-pounder anti-tank guns and three artillery seventeen pounders were manhandled into position. Pick-axes poked and prodded into the tree roots. The signals officer got to work laying a telephone back across the plateau to the battalion rear headquarters with the Somersets.

Sturmmann Zemlitz was a runner with 10th SS. The heavy British artillery fire had made a hash of the telephone lines on the German side. They were using runners, and Zemlitz knew every metre of the little wood and the German slope. He had to, his life depended on it:

> When the Tommies got into *das Wäldchen der halben Bäume* we moved to our last line of retreat. It was a dry stone wall overgrown with bushes, about a hundred metres further down the slope. It gave good cover and a good field of fire. Behind that ditch the slope ran

* A Canadian officer serving with the British Army under the Canloan scheme.

> on downhill for a thousand yards without a scrap of cover. We always said that we would have to hold that ditch or die in the attempt. Tommy never got that far.[6]

The evening light was fading rapidly. The Churchill tanks clanked back across the plateau, avoiding the stretcher parties and the wounded. Tanks don't fight at night. At least that is what the British Army manuals said : the night was the time for refuelling and maintenance.

The Cornishmen did not have to wait long. A sudden deluge of bombs and shells warned of the counter-attack coming in. Major Roberts, in the ditch cutting across the middle of the wood, could hear the shouted orders of the sergeant and corporal section commanders: 'Hold your fire! – Not yet! – Hold it!' then the nagging rat-ta-tats cut through the damp air of the approaching night. It was an attack by the German infantry dug in close by. It was beaten back, and when the defenders brought down the defensive artillery fire the attackers disappeared. The DCLI got to work again with picks and shovels, and in the near darkness they dug in like mad, sweating to get below ground. Time was not on their side.

Waiting and watching at the foot of the German slope was Untersturmfuehrer (Lieutenant) Martin Schroif. He had been there in his Tiger tank since midday. The heavy panzers had been withdrawn from the summit to avoid the British artillery fire. He had heard the shell fire rise in a great crescendo and had watched as the hilltop disappeared in great clouds of dust and smoke.

> I saw panzer grenadiers coming back down the slope and I then knew that the British must have attacked again and that we would be sent to drive them back. It was almost dark when the order came. On the right I could see the Tigers of No 1 Company already moving on to the slope. My objective was the Kastenwäldchen. We got to within about three hundred metres of it. I halted the company and opened fire. I pushed forward on the left into a hollow in the ground. We couldn't have been more than a hundred metres away. We fired with machine-guns and sent high explosive into the tree tops. Machine-gun fire rattled on the armour and we could see the muzzle flashes of the anti-tank guns.

The 10th SS Frundsberg Division had not waited. It was important not to allow the British to dig in with anti-tank guns. The panzer grenadiers were attacking with the Tiger tanks and two companies of 9th SS under command.

It was confusion that dominated this battle on the top of the hill. At night darkness and fear are natural partners. An exploding shell is a flash of blinding light, a crack of doom, and a shower of sparkling red-hot splinters. Battle is fought in a gigantic display of death-dealing fireworks. Tank crew are blind but for the flashes of light that throw everything into startled view. It is a brave man who will man an anti-tank gun kneeling in a shower of splinters showering down from the tree tops.

Casualties were heavy on both sides. The German infantry could not get forward through the heavy and accurate British artillery fire : the Tiger tanks feared to move closer without infantry protection. The stalemate was broken when it was discovered that the British were not holding the front edge of the wood. The panzer grenadiers took it over. The Tiger tanks moved forward with them.

One of the German tanks got to within fifteen yards of the British command post. Major Roberts and Sergeant Hill tackled it with a PIAT, but the bomb failed to explode. The German tank then moved off. 'Others, however, continued manoeuvring all over the battalion area and having, as they doubtless believed, cleared the wood, they came up over the crest of the ridge on either side of the orchard and started moving down the northern slopes.'[32]

It must have been two of these Tigers that crossed the plateau and moved down the British slope, moving blindly into the trenches of the Wiltshires. They did not open fire and no one thought they could be the enemy until Major Jeans saw the black cross. One Tiger crashed past Private Pipe, upsetting his mug of tea. It roared, a great blob in the darkness, 'moving in the direction of the Somersets'.

> I dreamt I was in a tropical forest and huge trees were crashing down on me.
>
> 'Are you alright, sir? Are you alright?'
>
> It was the corporal. A Tiger tank had come through the hedge and gone right over me, crushing my compass and binoculars which were laid out by my side. It had halted not far away – a darker patch in the night. I called for a two-inch mortar flare and took up the No 1 position on the gun.

Alas for Captain Perks's chance of knocking it out, the mortar flares had been left behind. The Tiger clanked uncertainly away into the night.

By midnight the battle for the little wood had settled down uncomfortably with the Cornish Light Infantry much reduced in numbers. They were holding one half of the wood and the panzer grenadiers were a hundred yards away along the bottom hedge. An optimistic report that the Kastenwäldchen was in German hands had sent the Tiger tanks back down the hill. Panzer Group West received a report that Hill 112 had been recaptured.

Just before midnight the commander of the 9th SS Hohenstaufen Panzer Grenadier Regiment arrived with the news that the divisional columns were meeting head-on with supply vehicles moving back from the front. In many of the narrow country lanes there was no room to pass. The panzer grenadiers had taken to their feet and were marching the last seven kilometres.

Battle and disorganisation follow each other just as night follows day. As at Maltot, so at the little wood on top of the hill, but with the added disadvantage that enemy bombardment and counter-attack had ushered in darkness to compound the confusion and uncertainty. The Cornishmen had been given no time to sort themselves out: one company was still missing and another was so weak from casualties that it was unable to take over the front edge of the wood as had been arranged. The battalion commander had about three hundred infantrymen; he had the battalion six-pounder anti-tank guns and four seventeen pounders of the Royal Artillery. It was very dark. There had been no chance to examine the lie of the land. The enemy was close by, with German machine-guns hammering the darkness with nervous strings of tracer from the far end of the wood.

All night long the artillery fire from both sides plastered the hill. 'We got no sleep,' said one of the panzer crewmen who was sitting it out at the foot of the hill. Zemlitz, the runner from 10th SS, said he went to sleep despite the continuous shell fire, he was so exhausted: 'One of our mortar sections, firing at the greatest possible elevation into the little wood, gave it everything, but the *Engländer* had moved in in strength.'[6]

The Duke of Cornwall's Light Infantry hung on, wondering what the dawn would bring. About three o'clock in the morning the panzer grenadiers of the 9th SS Hohenstaufen Division arrived and dug in on the German slope. Like the Cornishmen, they had had no sleep for over twenty-four hours.

It was the British who attacked first. With the first streaks of dawn fifteen Sherman tanks came suddenly into view from behind the British crest. They roared over the road, past the calvary cross, and on along the track of the ancient Roman road to the little wood. The Scots Greys, for it was they, were working on the theory that the faster they went the less likely was the enemy to turn them into 'Ronson Lighters'.*

They were answering the call of Lieutenant-Colonel James for help in turfing those German machine-gunners out of the bottom end of the wood. It didn't take them long. The Germans had adopted their usual defence: small forward outposts with the bulk of the troops and the panzers held hidden on the reverse slope.

The growing light of dawn revealed a greater danger. Lieutenant-Colonel James had climbed a tall tree. He could see the low ground beyond: 'Enemy infantry in large numbers forming up to attack!' was his shouted warning. He remained at his dangerously exposed vantage point to shoot the British artillery on to the target.

Back on the crest overlooking the village of Esquay an observation officer of the 94th Field Artillery was excitedly shouting orders to his battery five miles back at Cheux. The western slope of 112 was alive with German infantry and panzers.

The Germans attacked at 0615 hours. By that time the hill had all but disappeared in the smoke and dust of the artillery fire.

Leading the attack from the south was the company of Tiger tanks commanded by Untersturmfuehrer Martin Schroif. In a series of bounds, one lot of panzers covering the others, they climbed up the slope in a hail of shellfire. They rolled on past the panzer grenadiers, who looked up with unshaven, dusty sweat-covered faces and waved as the Tigers roared on. They were happy in the knowledge that they were not alone, that the panzers would sort it out for them. Schroif was three hundred yards from the Kastenwäldchen, where he had been during the attack the night before. Through the dust and smoke he saw the vague shapes of two Shermans. He fired twice in rapid succession and knocked them both out. He looked at his watch. It was twenty-minutes to seven. Shellfire was falling. The British were mixing in more smoke. He pushed on towards the edge of the wood, where he knocked out a third Sherman tank and put several anti-tank guns out of action. Unterscharfuehrer (Corporal) Winter in Panzer No 232 was hit by an anti-tank gun firing from the northern edge of the plateau.

Tigers were also leading the attack up the hill from the Esquay side, using a sunken lane which gave some cover. A British spotting plane, a Lysander, was now circling in the skies above, sending targets back to the artillery. Within minutes a great barrage of shells had almost blotted out the slope. Trautmann, a wireless operator in one of the Tigers, has described the attack:

* Ronson Lighter – a cigarette lighter fuelled by petrol. A name given by tank crew to the Sherman tank, which usually burst into flames when hit.

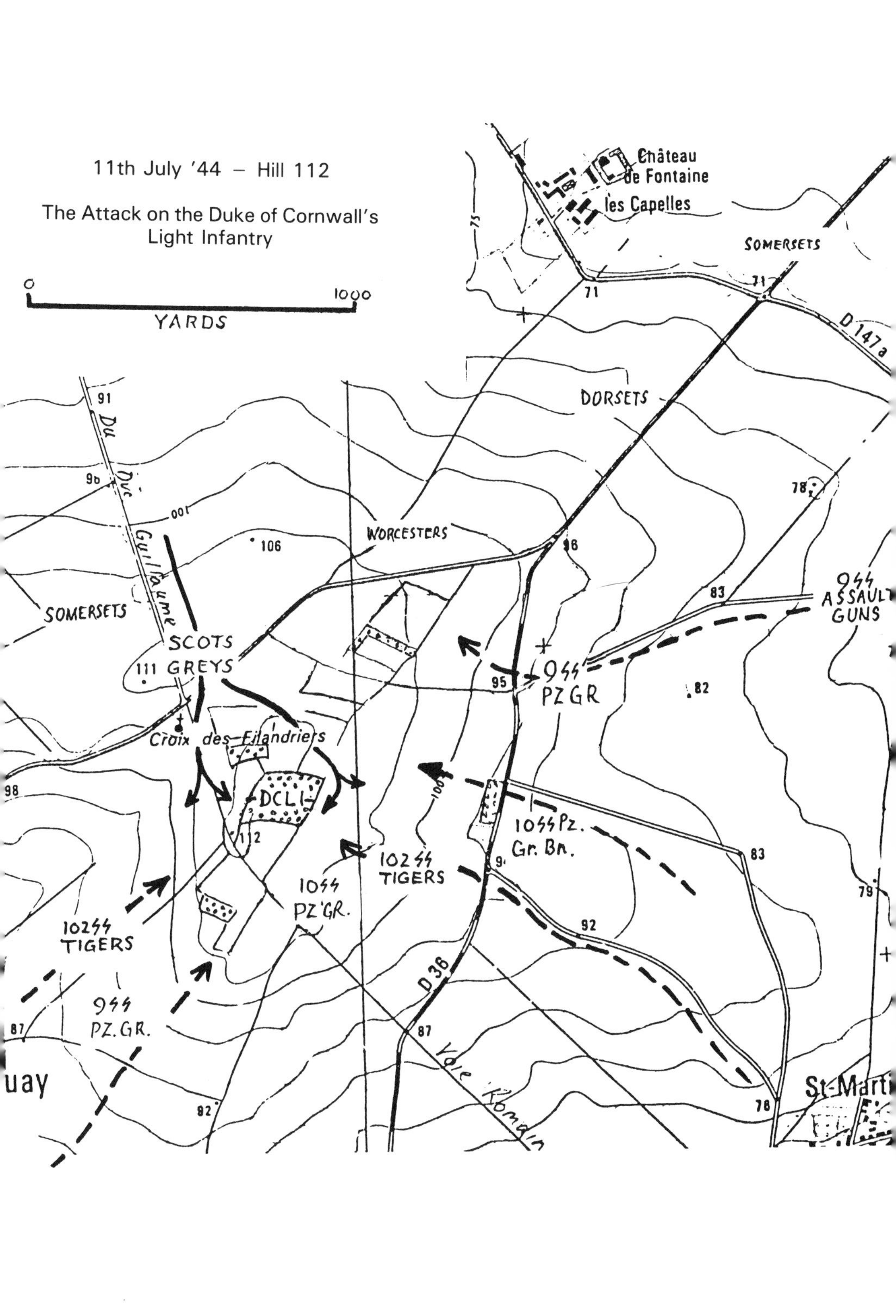
11th July '44 – Hill 112
The Attack on the Duke of Cornwall's Light Infantry
0
1000
YARDS
Château de Fontaine les Capelles
SOMERSETS
D 147a
DORSETS
Du Duc Guillaume
WORCESTERS
106
SOMERSETS
SCOTS GREYS
111
9SS PZ GR
9SS ASSAULT GUNS
Croix des Filandriers
DCLI
112
10SS Pz. Gr. Bn.
10SS TIGERS
10SS PZ'GR.
10SS TIGERS
9SS PZ.GR.
D 36
Voie Romain
St-Marti
uay

> . . . shells were exploding on the hull and turret; they were breaking off the branches in the tree tops! Our panzer grenadiers couldn't even raise their heads. Many brave comrades were left dead on the slopes.[28]

This advance from the west brought the German tanks to the large paddock extending beyond the wood. It was here that the remnants of the 'lost' company of the Duke of Cornwall's Light Infantry had dug-in. Wireless Operator Trautmann continues his account:

> On our left was an enclosure where our opponents were trying to bring an anti-tank gun into action. The crew was frantically pulling down the fence, and it was here that they suffered their first casualties. Brave they were, those Anglo-Saxons! In the meantime we had worked our way closer, and we quickly made the manhandling of that dark-brown gun a superfluous exercise![28]

As the Tiger tank worked its way past the paddock and the wood beyond, it was fired at and hit several times by anti-tank guns. None of them penetrated. The Cornishmen were learning the dangerous way that they were wasting their time firing a six-pounder anti-tank gun at a Tiger tank. Neither this gun nor the 75 mm gun of a Sherman would penetrate the front armour of a Tiger, even at very close range.

The British were sending supplies across the plateau and bringing back the wounded. To hide this from the enemy they had laid a thick smoke screen. The Tiger tank pushed on cautiously:

> This smoke must come to an end soon – suddenly we were through! Scarcely a hundred yards in front of us the Tommies were getting out. Trucks and carriers were curving this way and that, loading and unloading. Our commander came through on the intercom: 'Armour-piercing-fire when ready! Hull machine-gun – fire when ready!' Two Shermans were standing on guard directly in front of us. Even as they were traversing their guns we sent them up in flames. All the time our company commander was coming through on the radio: 'Pull back immediately! Pull back! Pull back level with the company!'[28]

The Scots Greys had lost five of their Shermans. They were hopelessly outnumbered and outgunned by far heavier tanks. Only the Sherman Firefly with the seventeen-pounder gun had any chance at all against a Tiger.* They retreated back over the British crest. From hull-down positions they continued to give what support they could.

The Cornwalls were on their own again. The battalion dead lay everywhere. Amongst them was Lieutenant King killed whilst standing on an embankment to direct the artillery fire, hit, it seems, by shrapnel from the barrage he had himself brought down. Little could be done for the wounded. The Bren carriers had been destroyed whilst trying to get them back to safety. Just one of the Tiger tank companies claimed in its war diary to have destroyed eight of them. The same company claimed also the destruction of three anti-tank guns. Destroyed or not, it made little difference to the Cornishmen, who were unable to man them in the withering fire of the enemy panzers. Many anti-tank crewmen lay dead or wounded.

The little wood was a conspicuous landmark, perched on top of the hill on the enemy side. It was a convenient size for the artillery to neutralise and steadily blow to pieces: 'Their shells burst amongst the trees, throwing splinters downwards and searching out the narrow slits without headcover which was all in the way of defences that the troops had been able to dig for themselves'.[32] They watched from these holes in the ground, bleary-eyed from lack of sleep, nerves twisted to the last turn, as one great Tiger tank after the other prowled round and round, throwing high-explosive into what was left of the trees and machine-gunning anything that looked suspicious. It seemed to them that all was lost. It was only a matter of time. They would be overrun.

But the attacking panzer grenadiers, too, were in a bad state. They had been caught in the open by the killing power of the British artillery, 'defensive fire such as we East Fronters had never known; the Russians had never as many guns as this'.[28]† The slopes leading up to the Kastenwäldchen were covered with German dead and wounded. The Tiger tanks might roam at will around the wood; only the panzer grenadiers could take it over. They were decimated, disorganised and demoralised, unable to move. Stalemate. The Germans were pulling back to think again.

It was as the fierce battle was ebbing away that word of the death of Lieutenant-Colonel James was passed from slit trench to slit trench. 'The CO has had it!' Gone was the example and inspiration that had done so much to keep these men going during the long night and morning of battle. He had climbed a tree. A burst of fire from a machine-gun

* One Sherman in each troop of four was a Firefly.

† Fey, 102 SS Heavy Panzer Battalion.

Panzer grenadiers under shell fire.

had hit him in the neck. He had fallen to the ground; almost beheaded.

Confidence and courage are to a surprising extent transmittable: so is fear. And there was plenty of reason for fear. Dead bodies of the defenders lay everywhere: in slit trenches, beneath the trees and out in the open. Over two hundred men had been wounded. When a rumour went around that a withdrawal had been ordered there were those who were in no mood to question it. They were getting out were they? About time too! Some tried to stop the rot, and the men dug in at the far end of the paddock remained in their trenches, either unaware of the departure elsewhere or doubtful about the authority to leave.

The Somersets watched as the groups of unshaven and exhausted soldiers trickled back through their positions:

'Eh, Sarge! Look at this bloody shower, then!'

To the British infantryman 'shower' was a name that he gave to all groups of soldiers except those of his own particular lot. But this bedraggled mob drifting back through the positions of the Somersets was not undeserving of the description. Lieutenant-Colonel Lipscombe of the Somersets took over. He was, in the words of one of his soldiers, 'a most remarkable and splendid man'. He rallied the exhausted Cornwalls, he turned their courage back to the sticking point, and he divided them into company groups; they numbered little more than a hundred men all told.

They set off back up the slope under the command of Major Roberts, crossed the road, went past the wayside calvary, and moved along the track of the old Voie Romaine, back to that fateful little wood. They were going back to fight on. There were some who would not come out again.

They found the wood as they had left it, except for six panzer grenadiers who had found refuge there and gave themselves up.

It was the destruction of the anti-tank defence that had most disturbed the Cornishmen. Captain Perks of the Somersets was sent back with them to see what he could do about it:

> I found three guns left behind. One was well forward with the platoon that had stayed. I went to look at it and was heavily cursed by the platoon commander, who didn't relish movement in that area. This gun had been knocked out.* I found two other guns in the woods, complete with sights and firing mechanisms, but no crews. I got only one volunteer. He had never touched a six-pounder before.

* This was the platoon in the paddock and the anti-tank gun that had that morning been knocked out by the Tiger.

This photograph of the 'little wood' was taken by Untersturmfuehrer Martin Schroif from the turret of his Tiger tank.

A panzer grenadier of the 9th SS Hohenstaufen Division takes cover just below the crest of Hill 112. The photograph was taken by Herbert Fuerbringer, who was wounded whilst taking part in the 9th SS counter-attack.

There was a rumour – false of course – that a Panther was approaching. So, using live ammunition I taught him how to load. I then got him to fell a small tree to get a better field of fire. Then the DCLI anti-tank gun commander turned up with two guns complete with crews. He didn't take kindly to my being there so I returned to my own lot, but not before I had broken open a fourteen-man pack of rations and given my volunteer all the cigarettes.

Herbert Fuerbringer was sitting in a cellar in the village of Avenay. He was a panzer grenadier with the 19th SS Panzer Grenadier Regiment. The only survivor from a machine-gun crew knocked out ten days earlier in the attack on Cheux, he was now a runner with Battlegroup Kriz. No word had reached the headquarters from the top of the hill, neither had any wounded come trickling back.

About midday Kriz ordered me forward to find out what was happening. He didn't want to risk unnecessary casualties by sending a patrol. I reached the road that skirted the top of the hill. It was hidden from the summit by a low embankment. I got to within twenty yards of the top. The sight was beyond all imagination. The dead, friend and foe, lay in masses on the open ground right up to the little wood. There the enemy was feverishly at work, digging in. I got back and reported to Kriz. At 1400 hours* we were ordered to attack. The 9th SS Panzer Regiment and guns from the anti-aircraft battalion were to support us. We advanced. Our own shells were falling all around us: never have I wanted it so much to stop. Then came the British artillery fire. Shell splinters were flying, smoke and powder drifted in the haze of a sweltering afternoon – not a cloud in the sky. The air was putrid with the smell of decomposing corpses. Our lot had got into the near side of the wood – what was left of it! I had almost got there when I heard another lot of shells. I ran – a jump this way and that – broken branches in the way – I fell nose down into the dirt. 'This way!' it was the voice of the sergeant. 'We're over here!' The shell fell as I was getting up. I went head-first into a trench. I had been hit in the leg. My comrades stopped the bleeding. 'That's it!' said the sergeant. 'You'll have to go back down the hill. Leave your ammunition. We're going to need that.' That was the last I saw of them.[16]

* 1500 hours British Army time.

Obersturmfuehrer (Lieutenant) Froehlich was commanding ten assault guns of the 9th SS Panzer Regiment:

> We had moved up the hill from Maltot and attacked early in the afternoon. Three of the guns were knocked out and three others received direct hits. The crews suffered heavy losses.

Sturmmann Zemlitz had come up the hill with the Tiger tanks:

> When they reached our position by the dry stone wall I jumped down, landing at the feet of Obersturmfuehrer Bramersdorf, our adjutant. 'Zemlitz – counter-attack!' he said. 'We're going to retake the wood.' We ran along one ditch and into another which led towards the corner of the little wood. I was behind him and there were four more behind me. That's all there were. He was first out of the ditch. We gave him covering fire as he ran with long strides towards the wood. Meanwhile the battle was raging and tanks were burning. We reached the wood with our panzers. But Bramersdorf was nowhere to be seen. . . He must have run straight into the arms of the *Engländer*.'[6]

For the handful of Cornishmen left to hold the wood this new attack by 9th SS marked the end of the battle. A great storm of mortar bombs and shells had howled down on them. When the German assault guns drove up and raked the wood with their fire from the lower ground the anti-tank gunners were unable to depress their guns enough to fire back. A seventeen-pounder was manhandled into a better position under cover of smoke; it was quickly smashed into silence.

A message was sent back with the adjutant. The situation was serious. The end was near. Permission was requested to withdraw. No reply came back. German panzers and guns continued to lob shells into the wood. Casualties increased, amongst them was the commander, Major Roberts. Major Fry, the only senior officer left, sent a second messenger. Still no reply came back. Fry took it upon himself to save what was left of them. Smoke was put down to cover a withdrawal. The bleary-eyed, stubble-chinned and utterly exhausted remnant of a proud county regiment got out with the wounded as best they could. Left behind were the bodies of ninety-three of their comrades. The total casualties in fifteen hours of battle came to three hundred and twenty. The regimental history notes with pride that only one man was taken prisoner.

9th SS panzer grenadiers charging across the top of Hill 112. Note the air-burst in the sky on the right.

Sherman tanks of the 4th Armoured Brigade knocked out in battle for the 'little wood'. The one in the foreground has had the turret blown off.

The 9th and 10th SS had forced the British to give up the Kastenwaeldschen; but they had been attacking all along the front. Their orders were to regain all the positions lost the previous day. They failed.

That night Hans Greisinger was with the panzer grenadiers holding the southern edge of the plateau :

> We were on the left, next to the shell-shattered Kastenwaeldschen. Tommy came twice in the darkness with shock troops but we were able to drive him off. One of the attackers was hit and burned to death before he could get his flame-thrower going. When we tried to contact our neighbours on the other side of the wood we found nothing there. They had cleared off without telling us.[16*]

The 'shock troops' were the Somersets, who had pushed forward in the hope of establishing themselves on top of the plateau. It remained a no man's land, with the British dug in along the northern edge and the Germans opposite them along the southern.

At half past seven that evening General Eberbach had spoken to Bittrich, the commander of the II SS Panzer Corps, on the telephone:

> On no account must Hill 112 be given up: it is the pivot for the whole front. We might be able to do without Eterville, but we must hang on to Hill 112.[17]

The counter-attack on Eterville had failed. 10th SS had attacked throughout the night of the 10th/11th. In a night of screaming mortar bombs and cascading phosphorus, of blinding flashes of automatic fire and of confusion and doubt, the 9th Cameronians had stood firm despite the loss of one company headquarters and the crews of three RA anti-tank guns, all presumably put in the bag. 10th SS renewed the attack just after dawn; it was forced to withdraw, leaving two panzers and many dead on the battlefield.

The offensive of the 43rd Wessex Division was finished. At the time it seemed just another failure. Now one can see what an impossible task had faced those civilian soldiers of Wessex in what was their first major battle.

'It must be admitted,' writes the historian of the division, 'that the German armour was less vulnerable than our own.' One takes note of the soft negative. Tank crew facing the enemy with an inferior gun and

* Greisinger in *Der Freiwillige*, Mai 1975.

Two photographs of Hill 112 after the battle.

inferior armour were more positive: 'Bloody Ronson lighters! No bloody good mate!' And the infantryman, looking around in vain for a sight of 'big brother', would have agreed. 'Well, that's what the balls-up at Maltot was all about, wasn't it!'

In all battles brave men go unrecognised. At the end of the chapter let us look back at one of them...

That little wood on Hill 112, stretching splintered and shattered tree trunks gauntly into the sky, was as forlorn and dangerous a battlefield as North-West Europe was to see. Nothing had gone right. The sweet-sick smell of battle hung in the atmosphere. Abandoned equipment, shattered guns and tanks littered the area. There were dead bodies, too. Exhausted by the din and stress of continuous battle, well into a second day without sleep, the Cornishmen were in no mood to welcome the strange officer from another regiment who had arrived looking for men to man the anti-tank guns. In this wood it was certainly the most dangerous job of all. Only one man came forward. A private soldier. He had never fired the gun before, but he would have a go. 'I have always regretted,' said Captain Perks, 'that I never recorded his name.' Let us hope that he lived long enough to enjoy those cigarettes from the fourteen-man pack.

CHAPTER FOURTEEN

Attrition

> Despite heavy losses yesterday, the British are preparing to attack again at Hill 112. They are determined to seize this key position.[17]

General Eberbach of Panzer Group West was worried. His panzer troops had suffered 'high and bloody' losses on Hill 112. At midday on the 11th July he spoke of his concern to Field-Marshal Rommel on the telephone.

He stressed the crisis arising from lack of replacements for men lost in battle. The time had surely come to consider closing down military teaching establishments to provide men for the battle front. In only two weeks of fighting 1st SS Panzer Division had lost 1,441 men, the Hohenstaufen Division had lost 1,891 and the Frundsberg had lost 2,289. The Hitler Youth, in battle since the second day of the invasion, had losses of over six thousand and was now a division in name only. The Waffen SS recruitment office had told him that there were only two thousand three hundred SS replacements in the pipe-line for those divisions and no more in the foreseeable future. The daily losses in the present battle were so high that divisions would soon be worn down beyond recovery. Eberbach asked whether it would not be possible to make up the strength of the SS panzer divisions from the pool of Wehrmacht replacements.

Too few soldiers to replace those lost was a British problem too. General Ronald Adam, Adjutant General, had arrived in Normandy from the War Office with a sombre warning. If British infantry losses continued at the same rate, then in three weeks, perhaps a month, the pool of trained infantry replacements would be dry. The British Second Army would then have to break up some of its divisions in order to keep others up to strength. Montgomery would find himself with a British army that was getting smaller.

It was not difficult to see why. In just two weeks of battle the British VIII Corps alone had lost over seven thousand men. Less than ten percent, one might say. But of every hundred soldiers lost eighty were infantrymen. Two infantry divisions, the 15th Scottish and the 43rd Wessex, accounted for five thousand of the casualties, and there had been heavy infantry casualties in 11th Armoured Division also. And even within the infantry battalion, the casualties were heavily concentrated in the rifle companies. The War Office had found out too late that war in the mid-twentieth century could not be won by aeroplanes and tanks alone. The British had trained too few infantrymen. Now that the battle had hardened into a slogging match, the infantryman, with only his khaki uniform to protect him, was finding it difficult to stay alive. With so many troops, so much armour and so many guns locked in battle in such a small area heavy losses were inevitable.

Time was running out for the British. It was at times of crisis that Montgomery's unflappability proved an invaluable asset. The American drive to obtain a good start-line for the breakout in the west was one week old. It had made little progress. It was a worried Bradley that had met with Montgomery and Dempsey, the British commander, to discuss the situation. 'Take all the time you need, Brad,' had been Montgomery's reassuring reply to Bradley's explanation of his difficulties. The Americans were fighting in very difficult country, were up against some first-class German infantry formations, and were suffering heavy casualties. Dempsey was told that the British would have to keep the pressure up, would have to keep hitting at the Germans, would have to ensure that the panzer divisions were kept tied up on the Caen front.

*

The battle started up again at Hill 112 on the night of the 15th. The Scotsmen were back. Our old friend Sergeant Jimmy Blair was there with the Glasgow Highlanders, but there were new faces, young nineteen-year-olds had arrived as replacements. Not enough, however, to bring the battalion up to strength. It was organised into three companies instead of the usual four. During a hot and sticky afternoon they had marched across the old battlefield, through the dust and debris of Cheux and Colleville and past 'Dead Cow Corner', the fiercest pong north of the Odon, and at eleven-thirty that night they had attacked from south of Baron.

In a weird glimmer of searchlights reflected from the clouds, in a great din of artillery and mortar fire, Jimmy Blair found himself in battle on the road from the wayside calvary towards the crossroads at le Bon Repos in a nightmare of fire and flame. Crocodiles were spitting out their vicious tongues, leaving hedgerows ablaze and turning trees into bright torches. The corn was burning, pools of flame danced on the roadway. Tracer curved in strings across the sky as the Luftwaffe put in a brief appearance. The Germans were being burned out of their positions. Silhouette figures darted this way and that; impossible to tell friend from foe.

By midnight the le Bon Repos crossroads was in Scottish hands. It was the sign for the whole western side of the corridor to erupt into battle.

The top of Hill 112 was not being attacked. It was screened off from the battle with explosive and smoke shells. The Tiger tanks would not find that out until later. They were on stand-to, half-way up the slope :

> Schroif's voice came over the intercom : 'Panzers advance immediately. Draw level with the infantry positions!' What was the use of that? Nobody could see in all that dust and smoke where the front line was, or even where the other panzers were. Piller's voice came through over the network. 'What am I supposed to do? There's thick smoke all round me. I can't see a thing!' He sounded so helpless – we all laughed. It was past midnight* when the din of battle at last began to die down. Had our defence been overrun? We stared into the darkness ready to give Tommy a good welcome. Or had the attack been repulsed. Suddenly I felt desperately tired.†

On the other side of the hill, near Baron, Lieutenant Robert Woollcombe had watched the Moaning Minnies fall 'like giant cigarette stubs' out of the sky and explode into fountains of phosphorus on the start-line. He had felt certain he would be killed in this battle. Many others were, including the brigadier, with a direct hit on his headquarters, but not Woollcombe, who that night led men of the King's Own Scottish Borderers forward onto the slopes of neighbouring hill 113. The company fighting strength had sunk to seventy-five men. Less than half that number would come back down the hill a few days later. It would be all that was left of those who had trained so hard and so long together in the United Kingdom.

The British were gaining ground along the whole western side of

* Past one o'clock British army time.

† Oberscharfuehrer Ernst Streng, Tiger tank commander with the 102 SS Heavy Tank Battalion.

the corridor. 9th SS Panzer Regiment, just taken out of the line for maintenance, was rushed back to counter-attack with SS panzer grenadiers and fusiliers of the Wehrmacht infantry division:

> The British defended with great obstinacy. We knocked out eighteen of their tanks and put down heavy concentrations of artillery fire; only then did we make slow progress at Bougy. Enemy tanks continued to fight on with skill from the sunken roads and hedgerows.[33]

This German tribute to the tenacity and skill of the 153rd Regiment Royal Armoured Corps, who were supporting the infantrymen of the 8th Royal Scots, was bought with heavy casualties: twenty-six Churchill tanks knocked out, thirty-nine tank crew killed, fifty-seven wounded, including the commander. Bougy remained in British hands, as did, also, Gavrus, which the British had earlier captured.

At Evrecy, however, there was no success. First the Scotsmen failed, then a brigade of Royal Welch Fusiliers.* It suffered such crippling losses – including all three commanding officers – that the battalions were afterwards placed in different brigades to avoid such heavy casualties being concentrated in one regiment in future.

Field-Marshal Rommel had reported to Hitler that after taking Caen the Allies would advance on Paris. That report, intercepted and decoded by Ultra, had been read by Montgomery. His bluff was succeeding. He would now have to keep the Germans thinking that way. He worked out his plan for a new major British offensive.

Once again it was General O'Connor who was chosen to lead. But it was the White Knight of VIII Corps with a difference. To keep infantry casualties down, 'Goodwood', as the offensive was called, would be a drive forward from east of Caen by a phalanx of three armoured divisions. O'Connor left the 15th Scottish and the 43rd Wessex divisions at Hill 112 under command of XII Corps. He took his corps troops and 11th Armoured Division to the other side of Caen. The Guards Armoured Division and The Desert Rats were to enter the battle as the advance gained ground.

At the other end of the front the Americans were battling to win the town of St Lô, and Bradley, the American commander, reported that he would be ready to start the long awaited breakout offensive on the 19th. Montgomery ordered Goodwood to start on the 18th. It would

* 53rd Welsh Division – under command of the 15th Scottish.

A battalion commander of the Royal Welch Fusiliers gives orders to his officers for the attack on Evrecy on 16th July 1944. The attack was repulsed with heavy losses.

Evrecy.

tie the German panzer divisions down at Caen, prevent their being switched to the American front.

Things started to happen. On the 17th Field-Marshal Rommel was inspecting the defences of the Panzer Group when his staff car was shot up by a marauding 'Jabo'. Rommel was badly wounded and out of the battle. At ten minutes past ten that evening, Army Group 'B' telephoned Eberbach to say that Field-Marshal von Kluge had stepped in to take Rommel's place. He would be both Commander in the West and of Army Group 'B', fighting the battle in Normandy.

The next morning, the 18th, two thousand Allied bombers turned the German defences east of Caen into a cratered wasteland. 'Pip' Roberts and 11th Armoured Division drove into the dust and smoke for almost five miles and emerged to find they had still not penetrated the German defences. They fought a lone battle for much of the day without even the support of their own infantry. The surviving tanks were brought to a halt on the Bourguébus ridge. They were eight miles into enemy territory. They no longer had the support of the artillery, for they had moved beyond its range. A pall of black smoke hung in the sky behind them. The plain was strewn with burning wrecks. The division had lost one hundred and twenty-six tanks. The Guards and the Desert Rats were delayed by that curse of all the major British offensives in Normandy, the traffic jam. The Guards arrived in the afternoon and quickly lost sixty tanks; the Desert Rats arrived in the evening, too late to play any effective part in the battle.

It all proved to be in vain; the next day the Americans failed to attack at all. The breakout had been delayed by German resistance at St Lô.

Goodwood was seen everywhere as a disaster. The British had 'ballsed it up' again. War is a game of bluff. The underlying motive could not be revealed. Monty could hardly tell the British and Canadian troops that they were being sacrificed to help the Americans, even if it was for the common good.

Chief Big Wind must go! That was the verdict at Eisenhower's Allied headquarters, where Montgomery had made many enemies. Pressure was put on Churchill to remove him. But Monty proved to be a great survivor. There is irony in the knowledge that this clamour was loudest at a time when the tactical plan was at last moving towards success.

The German command was more worried than ever. Goodwood had destroyed the 16th Luftwaffe Field Division (infantry), and the 21st Panzer Division would only survive by taking the remnants of that division into its infantry regiment. The 12th SS Hitler Youth Division, just pulled out of the line to recuperate after many weeks of continuous battle and heavy losses, had been rushed back in to plug the gap. The 1st SS Adolf Hitler Division seemed to be suffering from the old soldier disease that was affecting the British desert veterans. Its counter-attack from the Bourguébus ridge had failed. The German command saw Goodwood as the Allied effort to break out of the Normandy strait-jacket. They were certain that it would be continued, with the main thrust south towards Falaise as a first objective. At midnight von Kluge was on the telephone to Hitler's headquarters. He wanted and got the release of the 116th Panzer Division. It was to move into defence south of Caen. Kluge also gave orders for the transfer of the 2nd Panzer Division from its position at Caumont, where it was facing the Americans. It, too, was to move to counter the British threat. All eyes were on the Caen front.

*

The worm's eye view of war went on at Hill 112:

> The infantry were down to eight men to a platoon and were very tired. They rested while we manned forward. posts and patrolled. It rained like hell for the first two days... The position was high ground, with a valley in front of us – a lousy place that stank to high heaven.[34]

The Seaforth Highlanders were still hopelessly under strength. They were in defence near le Valtru, where three weeks earlier so many of their men had been killed. They had still to recover from those losses. The men from an armoured car unit had been sent forward to help them out. Little wonder that the place 'stank to high heaven'. It was here that the big battle had taken place with the 9th SS Hohenstaufen Division. There were dead bodies in the hedges and rotting carcasses lying in no man's land, and they had been there for three weeks.

The 9th SS, too, had not recovered. With no hope in the foreseeable future of sufficient SS replacements to bring its six battalions of infantry up to strength, it had reorganised with only four.

The British front at Hill 112 still ran roughly along the line of road that crossed the summit from east to west. The main British positions were well back from the crest and hidden from enemy view, but the forward companies had outposts on the high ground and further forward where they could see the enemy and were themselves under observation. The artillery and mortars of both sides had been pounding the hill for four weeks.

The panzer grenadiers developed such a fear of the British artillery fire that they were ordering the observation posts for the artillery and mortars to keep away from them. They were convinced that the British were homing in on the wireless and fixing its position.

> It wasn't long before three enemy shells exploded very close to the dugout. It wasn't really a dugout, just a trench three feet deep, covered with planks and earth. There were two wireless operators inside, and a crawl trench led forward to the observer. He had to crawl back along the trench to give the fire orders. The fourth shell was a direct hit on the dugout. It killed all three of them.[6]

Sturmmann Zemlitz, the 10th SS runner who reported this incident, moved down from the hill with just forty-six survivors of the 3rd Battalion 22nd SS Panzer Grenadier Regiment. It was this battalion that had occupied the little wood when the Cornishmen abandoned it.

> We had twenty new runners one after the other. They were always being killed or wounded. Amongst them were two soldiers from an army mortar unit who, instead of three days arrest, had to spend a week with us.[6]

On 20th July the 53rd Welsh Division took over the British positions on the hill. An officer of the 2nd Monmouths has left this picture of life there :

> I don't think I ever heard a bird in Normandy, though I did see a dead one blasted in a hedge. Dust was part of the atmosphere – powdery white dust. Smell, too, was an element – a difficult smell to imagine and a nasty one to analyse, though it was the German side of 112 which was worse in that respect. Approaching the hill from the rear, by the much shelled Baron road, one could work forward by dusty hedgerows honeycombed with funk holes to a point where they stopped and one was confronted with the open hill itself. This was a parched, bald slope rising to a skyline over which an Air OP usually hummed, dipping and dodging in the sky. Towards this bare skyline went all manner of whispering shells, warbling mortar bombs and screaming missiles from our gun-lines in the rear. Back across

the summer skyline came the howling, rushing 'swoosh' of German shells and the occasional 'Moaning Minny'.[27]

Looking up at that artillery observation plane from a Tiger tank on the other side of the hill was Ernst Streng :

> That damned English crow is hanging in the sky again. Doesn't he know there's a war on? He's got a nerve, flying in curves and circles over the front like that! A machine-gun could easily bring him down. But nothing stirs in our front line. The infantryman there knows that the slightest sign of life will bring down the shells from the enemy batteries – and they will be bang on target. Throughout the intense heat of the July afternoon our infantry lie motionless in their holes in the ground, following with their eyes every movement in the sky above.

The most exposed and isolated of the British posts were those at the le Bon Repos crossroads and the Maison Blanche farm five hundred yards further up the hill. They had been captured a few nights earlier by the Glasgow Highlanders.

Some men from the Welch arrived one night and took over. With the light of dawn the Welshmen realised that they were in full view of the enemy who were in Esquay, four hundred yards down the road, and on the slopes on both sides. Any movement brought a sniper's bullet. They were imprisoned in their trenches all through the long summer day. Food in fourteen-man packs they collected at night. They tossed the tins from one trench to another, counted out the cigarettes and sweets, and looked thoughtfully at the sheets of toilet paper also provided, hoping that it would be only in the dark that the urge came to use it. Confined to their narrow trenches throughout the hours of daylight, they passed the time warming up the tins and making frequent brews of compo tea over the sickly fumes of a Tommy Cooker. From time to time there would be a diversion : the snout of a long 88 mm gun would appear over the bald hump of the hill and the turret of the Tiger tank that owned it would come slowly into view. A couple of rounds would swoosh past leaving a vacuum that took the breath away and threatened to collapse the lungs.

These Tommies who had pushed well forward into German territory and pinched the outposts were seen by the enemy as a provocation and a nuisance. 10th SS had taken over. They would do something about it. One afternoon they attacked with assault groups of panzer grenadiers,

Le Bon Repos.

six Tiger tanks and supporting artillery fire. The outpost at la Maison Blanche was quickly overrun. Some survivors escaped back over the crest to the safety of the British slope. The battle at le Bon Repos, however, went on until well into the night. No one came back from there.

On the 22nd Maltot was attacked and captured by the 4th and 5th Wiltshires supported by the 7th Royal Tanks. It was the Wiltshires who twelve days earlier had suffered heavy losses on the slopes of 112. The 7th Royal Tanks had supported the Glasgow Highlanders at Cheux, where eight of their tanks had been destroyed, and they had also been in the attack on the hill, where they lost six more.

Maltot was a terrible sight. The streets were blocked with debris. The stench was appalling. The blackened bodies of the dead of the Hampshires and Dorsets still lay where they had fallen twelve days earlier. They were in groups around the slit trenches they had started to dig. Little more than the top soil had been removed.

The wooded spur east of the village, which twelve days before had contained the panzers that had cut them down, was receiving the attention of the 4th Wiltshires. They ran into fierce resistance from a defended château. It was the German battalion headquarters and also its medical aid post. A medical orderly had come out with a white flag and requested permission to evacuate the large number of wounded. The request was refused. The garrison would have to surrender. With the tanks firing into the château at point-blank range the Wiltshires penetrated the ground floor only to be thrown back with casualties by a storm of fire coming from the upper storeys. It was only at dawn the next day that the Germans surrendered.

The Wiltshires took over five hundred prisoners in Maltot. The 5th Battalion lost sixteen men killed and seventy-two wounded. The losses of the 4th Battalion must have been similar.

Not for nothing did the men of the three battalions of Tiger tanks in Normandy refer to themselves as the 'Feuerwehr'. Whenever a crisis occurred the 'Fire Brigade' was rushed in. The 102 SS Tiger Battalion had been pulled back from 112 for much needed maintenance. Ernst Streng was with them when they downed tools and raced forward to plug the gap:

> Like great prehistoric monsters we roared on towards St Martin. The village was on fire; shells were flashing, flames and smoke were rising up, burning wood and debris were showering down into the narrow road. We were enveloped in dust and smoke. When we emerged into

'Maltot was a terrible sight. The Churchill tank is from the 7th Royal Tank Regimer

The Château.

German prisoners (27 Infantry Division) taken i Maltot.

the clearer air beyond, the *Engländer* saw us. Down came the fire curtain. It followed us as though we were a magnet. We picked up stragglers who had escaped from Maltot. We swung into a defensive line between Maltot and Feuguerolles. Behind us the panzers and assault guns of the 11 SS Panzer Corps were also arriving.

It was still light enough to see the church tower of Maltot poking above the line of trees. The sky beyond flickered red every time the English batteries fired their salvos. It was midnight when we were told that there would be no counter-attack. We didn't have enough infantry.

At ten o'clock the next morning English tanks came along the road leading to St Martin. In silence we watched them. Then we started the motors up, we traversed the turret and got on target. There was a great roar as the gun fired. A spear of flame shot up from one of the Churchills. Black smoke poured out. Then an explosion blew the turret and tracks into the air. Our company knocked out six of them.

That same evening, le Bon Repos, 'the quiet resting place' – what a misnomer that was proving to be – flared up once again in fierce battle. It was there that Sergeant Moppett's patrol was shot up after the night attack on Baron; two weeks later it was captured by the Glasgow Highlanders; then 10th SS recaptured it from the 5th Welch; now, as the daylight was fading, the 4th Welch were getting their own back. 'Well, we couldn't let them duff-up our boys like that, could we!' As a great weight of explosive dropped out of the evening sky two companies of angry men from the valleys of South Wales came rushing over the crest. Six crocodile flame-throwers added to the horror and increased the confusion by arriving as the Welshmen were turning the Germans out of their trenches. 'A Bren gunner has found two Germans hiding under a mattress in a trench. They won't come out so are ripped to pieces...'

It was all over in half an hour. One man staggered in with his wounded mate on his back, others were helping the walking wounded. For three weeks these men had seen friends killed and wounded by mortar and shell fire. For the first time they had been able to hit back.

The next day, the 24th, one of the Tigers in the Maltot area was knocked out. Streng had taken his panzer forward to relieve his friend Oberhuber:

I drove my Tiger alongside his. He was excited. Anti-tank guns had moved into positions in the woods opposite. Suddenly a fountain of dust shot up behind us. Where did that one come from? When a second shot threw up a spout of sand just in front it was no longer a joke. 'Anti-tank guns! – Start up! – Load HE!' A blinding flash shot from the side of Oberhuber's panzer. I felt the intense heat of the impact. There was a round black hole the thickness of a man's arm. The jolt had sent Oberhuber tumbling out of the turret. Hatches were flung open. Out scrambled the crew, terrified eyes in pale faces. Black smoke billowed out. 'Reverse! Reverse!' I shouted. Back we went, throttle wide open, engine roaring. I saw the other driver, waving a blood-covered stump with the hand hanging from a few shreds of flesh.

*

'It's not the big British attack. I'm certain of that. If it were we would be seeing a lot more activity in the air.[17]

It was 25th July. General Eberbach was talking to Field-Marshal von Kluge on the telephone. They were discussing the battle that had just flared up again on the bank of the Orne opposite Maltot. Kluge agreed, but stressed the importance of having everything ready:

Make sure that the counter-attack force is in the right place. There will be no time when the big attack comes in, and there must be no delay.[17]

Eberbach pointed out that the 116th Panzer Division was poised for action near Falaise and the 2nd Panzer Division would be arriving from Caumont that night.

That same morning, the Americans, at the other end of the front, had started the long awaited break-out effort in the west.

Cobra, as it was called, got off to a bad start. The Germans were unconcerned. It was well into the second day before the mood began to change. At half-past-nine that evening a message was flashed to Eberbach's headquarters: the 2nd Panzer Division was to get on the road that night and move west. At midnight a second message came: Was the 2nd Panzer Division on the way?

By the next morning the crisis had deepened. The 116th Panzer Division was also to move west with all possible speed. The Americans were on the rampage and would have to be stopped.

Field-Marshal von Kluge (1) talking to General Eberbach, who is wearing the black uniform of a panzer officer. The disfigurement of his face is the result of a war wound.

On the 30th the British launched a new offensive. The blow fell not at Caen where the Germans were expecting it, but in the centre of the Normandy front, at Caumont. To launch 'Bluecoat' the British Army had suddenly switched its weight from Caen to the boundary with the Americans. It had moved six divisions and two armoured brigades through the narrow country lanes at right angles to the congested roads supplying the front.

Spearheading this new offensive was none other than General Dick O'Connor with the White Knight of VIII Corps. The 11th Armoured Division had broken through along the boundary with the Americans, and the 15th Scottish and 43rd Wessex infantry* were advancing on the left.

Two days later the German Feuerwehr was on the move; the 102 SS Tiger Tank Battalion was pulling out from Hill 112 and hurrying to a new point of crisis. It was not alone. All night the roads leading west behind the German front were nose to tail with the panzers and halftracks of the II SS Panzer Corps. But it was not to stop the Americans, who were pushing tanks through the Avranches gap. It was to stop the British, who had torn a great hole in the centre. Daylight would find the 9th SS Hohenstaufen and 10th SS Frundsberg divisions back in battle with an enemy they thought they had left behind: the 15th Scottish, the 43rd Wessex and the 11th Armoured Division.

Complete victory in Normandy was less than three weeks away.

* Now with XXX Corps.

EPILOGUE

1944.

1984.

Epilogue

And what of Hill 112? Like the old soldier it simply faded away. On the night of 3rd/4th August patrols of the 53rd Welsh Division returned to report that Jerry had gone. That morning the dawn broke with an eerie silence and heavy scent of death. Stubble-chinned, dirty, dust-covered infantrymen emerged from holes in the ground and stretched themselves. It was good to be able to move freely again.

The German side of the hill was carnage. Bodies, blackened and blown up after weeks of exposure to the sun and the rain, lay everywhere unburied. Shattered and abandoned equipment littered the slopes. The hill was a graveyard of tanks, blackened, rusting hulks. There were mines too. A patrol went over the crest and down into Esquay village. Not a building remained standing. The roads were impassable with debris. Dead bodies in shallow graves had been uncovered by the shell fire. At le Bon Repos crossroads a padre was trying to identify bodies of men of the 5th Welch.

It was some days later, the sound of battle had moved far away, when a British army truck drove up to the top of the hill and some soldiers got out carrying a large board. In their caps was the badge of the Duke of Cornwall's Light Infantry. They erected a large signboard:

CORNWALL HILL

July 10th–11th 1944

The paint faded long ago and the wood weathered and fell to pieces. There stands in its place, not far from the calvary, which is still there, a granite monument to the men of the 43rd Wessex Division. If you look south from the monument you will be looking across the '44 no man's land of the summit, and you will see outlined against the sky the trees of that little wood where so many men died.

Source References

1 *Story of the 23rd Hussars* (BAOR 1945).
2 Churchill, W. S., *Closing of the Ring* (Cassell 1952).
3 Army Group of the North Ukraine, Order No 278/44, quoted in Tieke, W., *Im Feuersturm Letzter Kriegsjahre* (Munin 1975).
4 Woollcombe, R., *Lion Rampant* (Chatto & Windus 1955).
5 Schramm, P. E. (Ed.), *Kriegstagebuch des Oberkommandos der Wehrmacht 1944–1945* (Bernard & Graefe Verlag 1982).
6 Tieke, W., *Im Feuersturm Letzter Kriegsjahre* (Munin 1975).
7 Connell, J., *Wavell – Scholar and Soldier* (Collins 1969).
8 Grandais, A., *La Bataille du Calvados* (Presses de la Cité, 1973).
9 Meyer, H., *Kriegsgeschichte der 12. SS–Panzerdivision 'Hitlerjugend'* (Munin Verlag 1983).
10 Panzermeyer, *Grenadiere* (Schild Verlag 1957).
11 *Berichte Heeresgruppe B* (Militärarchiv, Freiburg).
12 Joscelyne, R., *'A' Squadron Diary – 7th Royal Tanks.*
13 McKee, A., *Caen: Anvil of Victory* (Souvenir Press Ltd.).
14 *Kriegstagebuch 7. Armee Ferngespraeche* (Militärarchiv, Freiburg).
15 Weidinger, O., *Division das Reich – Band V* (Munin Verlag 1982).
16 *Der Freiwillige* (Munin Verlag).
17 *Kriegstagebuch Panzergruppe West* (Militärarchiv, Freiburg).
18 Bell, N., *From the Beaches to the Baltic* (Gale & Polden).
19 Carell, P., *Sie Kommen!* (Gerhard Stellung Verlag).
20 Martin, H. C., *The History of the 15th Scottish Division 1939–1945* (Blackwood 1948).
21 Bevan, D. G., *The First and Second Northamptonshire Yeomanry 1939–1945* (Meyer 1946).
22 Brownlie, W. S., *The Proud Trooper* (Collins 1964).

23 Kemp, P. K., *History of the King's Shropshire Light Infantry (T.A.) 1795–1945* (Wilding 1955).
24 Baggaley, J. R. P., *The 6th (Border) Battalion the King's Own Scottish Borderers 1939–1945* (Berwick 1946).
25 Jackson, G. S., *Operations of the VIII Corps* (St Clements Press 1948).
26 *Kriegstagebuch 7. Armee* (Militärarchiv, Freiburg).
27 Brett, G. A., *History of The South Wales Borderers & The Monmouthshire Regiment Vol III* (Hughes 1954).
28 Fey, W., *Panzer im Brennpunkt der Fronten* (Lehmann's Verlag).
29 *History of the 4th Bn The Somerset Light Infantry (Prince Albert's) in the Campaign in North-West Europe June 1944–May 1945* (Phoenix Press).
30 Watkins, J. G. B., *From Normandy to the Weser* (Dorset Press).
31 Meredith, J. L. J., *The Story of the Seventh Battalion of the Somerset Light Infantry (Prince Albert's).*
32 Godfrey & Goldsmith, *The History of the Duke of Cornwall's Light Infantry 1939–1945* (Gale & Polden 1966).
33 *Tagesmeldungen der 9. SS–Panzerdivision* (Militärarchiv, Freiburg).
34 Kemsley & Riesco, *The 15th Scottish Reconnaissance Regiment* (White Swan Press, Bristol).
35 Cumberlege, G. (Ed.), *B.B.C. Report* (OUP 1946).
36 Lomax & de Courcy, *The History of the Welch Regiment 1919–1951* (Western Mail & South Wales Echo).
37 *Die Hellebarde – Nachrichten der Kameradschaftvereinigung Suchdienst Frundsberg*, Hannover.

Other Sources
Unpublished

War Diary of the 7th Battalion the Hampshire Regiment, British Archives, Kew, London.
Gefechtsbericht der 2. Kompanie s.SS–Pz.Abt 102.
Diary of Lieutenant Steel Brownlie, Fife & Forfar Yeomanry.
Diary of Lieutenant Steel Brownlie, Fife & Forfar Yeomanry.
Kampfraum Südwestlich Caen – unpublished account of Herr Ernst Streng.

Published

Calvocoressi, *Top Secret Ultra* (Cassell 1980).
Ellis, I. F., *Victory in the West* Vol I (HMSO 1962).
Essame, H., *The 43rd Wessex Division at War 1944–1945* (Clowes 1952).
E.W.I.P., *Taurus Pursuant* (BAOR 1945).
Hamilton, N., *Monty – Master of the Battlefield* (Hamish Hamilton 1983).
Hartwell, Pack & Edwards, *The Story of the Fifth Battalion The Dorset Regiment in North-West Europe* (Dorset Press).
How, J. J., *Normandy – the British Breakout* (Kimber 1981).
Irving, D., *The War Between the Generals* (Allen Lane 1981).
Lewin, R., *Ultra Goes to War* (Hutchinson 1978).
McMath, J. S., *The Fifth Battalion The Wiltshire Regiment in North-West Europe* (Whitefriars Press).
Parson, Robbins & Gilson, *The Maroon Square.*
Perrett, B., *Through Mud and Blood* (Hale 1975).
Wilmot, C., *The Struggle for Europe* (Collins 1952).

Index